DOVER · THRIFT · EDITIONS

Gunga Din and Other Favorite Poems

RUDYARD KIPLING

DOVER PUBLICATIONS, INC.
New York

DOVER THRIFT EDITIONS
Editor: Stanley Appelbaum

Copyright © 1990 by Dover Publications, Inc.
All rights reserved under Pan American and International
Copyright Conventions.

Published in Canada by General Publishing Company, Ltd.,
30 Lesmill Road, Don Mills, Toronto, Ontario.
Published in the United Kingdom by Constable and Company, Ltd.

This new anthology, first published by Dover Publications, Inc., in 1990, contains 44 poems reprinted from the following sources:

The Works of Rudyard Kipling [on spine: "Authorized Edition"]: *Departmental Ditties and Ballads and Barrack-Room Ballads,* Doubleday & McClure Company, N.Y., 1899.
The Seven Seas, Doubleday, Doran & Company, Inc., Garden City, 1928 (copyrights claimed: 1893, 1894, 1896 and 1905).
The Five Nations, Doubleday, Page & Company, N.Y., 1903.
The Mandalay Edition of the Works of Rudyard Kipling: Songs from Books/The Years Between and Parodies, Doubleday, Page & Company, Garden City, 1925 (copyrights claimed for *Songs from Books* extend from 1891 to 1912).
The Vampire, Woodward & Lothrop, Washington, D.C., 1898.
Recessional, The Hayes Lithographing Co., Buffalo, 1910.
The Absent-Minded Beggar, Brentano's, N.Y., 1900.
The Ladies' Home Journal, November 1911 issue.

The table of contents indicates the source volume of each poem. The "Note," "Notes to the Text" and alphabetical lists were prepared specially for the present anthology.

Manufactured in the United States of America
Dover Publications, Inc.
31 East 2nd Street
Mineola, N.Y. 11501

Library of Congress Cataloging-in-Publication Data

Kipling, Rudyard, 1865–1936.
Gunga Din and other favorite poems / Rudyard Kipling.
p. cm. — (Dover thrift editions)
ISBN 0-486-26471-8 (pbk.)
I. Title. II. Series.
PR4852 1990
821'.8—dc20   90-3685
CIP

Note

RUDYARD KIPLING (1865–1936) enjoys a firm reputation as a novelist, short-story writer and children's author. His poems, for all their technical solidity and variety, have rarely been accorded the same critical kudos. In their own day they were too popular with general readers to suit the academics; in our day their imperialism and antifeminism sometimes jar the reader. But, however rated, they remain an essential part of the Anglo-American heritage, and have been enormously influential on later writing of all types, not to mention the world of music and film. The number of well-known quotations they have added to our mental treasuries is truly surprising, as a careful reader of the present new selection will discover or rediscover.

The textual history of Kipling's poems is complex. They appeared in newspapers and magazines before being assembled into collections. These collections themselves were constantly enlarged and altered before being subsumed and totally reshuffled into various "inclusive" and "complete works" editions. Punctuation was in perpetual flux, the wording being much more stable. The texts here reprinted appear exactly as in the editions listed in the copyright statement in this volume (except for the correction of a few obvious errors). The poems are grouped according to the first collections into which they were gathered, and are arranged in the same order they had in those original collections. (The collection *Songs from Books* contained verse interpolations from a number of earlier prose volumes, which are also identified in the present table of contents.) The alphabetical lists of titles and first lines at the end of the book will facilitate the finding of any individual poem. The section "Notes to the Text" provides brief glosses and explanations, particularly of Anglo-Indian and military terms.

Contents

                                                                                   page

From *Departmental Ditties and Other Poems* (1886 ff.)
    A Legend of the Foreign Office   1
    The Story of Uriah   2
    My Rival   3
    The Betrothed   4

From *Ballads and Barrack-Room Ballads* (1892 ff.)
    The Ballad of East and West   6
    The Ballad of the King's Mercy   9
    The Ballad of the 'Bolivar'   12
    The Conundrum of the Workshops   13
    In the Neolithic Age   15
    The English Flag   16
    Tomlinson   18
    Danny Deever   22
    Tommy   24
    'Fuzzy-Wuzzy'   25
    Gunga Din   27
    Oonts   29
    The Widow at Windsor   30
    Mandalay   32
    Gentlemen-Rankers   33
    L'Envoi (The Long Trail)   35

From *The Seven Seas* (1896)
    McAndrew's Hymn   37
    Sestina of the Tramp-Royal   42
    'When 'Omer smote 'is bloomin' lyre'   44
    The Ladies   44
    The Sergeant's Weddin'   46
    The 'Eathen   47
    L'Envoi ('When Earth's last picture is painted')   50

From *The Five Nations* (1903)	
The Sea and the Hills	50
The White Man's Burden	52
Boots	53
From *Songs from Books* (1912 ff.)	
Cities and Thrones and Powers (from *Puck of Pook's Hill*, 1906)	54
Tarrant Moss (from *Plain Tales from the Hills*, 1888)	55
A Song to Mithras (from *Puck of Pook's Hill*)	56
Hadramauti (from *Plain Tales from the Hills*)	56
The Law of the Jungle (from *The Second Jungle Book*, 1895)	57
If— (from *Rewards and Fairies*, 1910)	59
'I keep six honest serving-men' (from *Just So Stories*, 1902)	60
The Song of the Little Hunter (from *The Second Jungle Book*)	61
Blue Roses (from *The Light That Failed*, 1890)	61
Mother o' Mine (from *The Light That Failed*)	62
From Miscellaneous Sources	
The Vampire (1897)	62
Recessional (1897)	63
The Absent-Minded Beggar (1899)	64
The Female of the Species (1911)	66

A Legend of the Foreign Office

This is the reason why Rustum Beg,
   Rajah of Kolazai,
Drinketh the "simpkin" and brandy peg,
   Maketh the money to fly,
Vexeth a Government, tender and kind,
Also—but this is a detail—blind.

Rustum Beg of Kolazai—slightly backward Native State—
Lusted for a C. S. I.—so began to sanitate.
Built a Gaol and Hospital—nearly built a City drain—
Till his faithful subjects all thought their ruler was insane.

Strange departures made he then—yea, Departments stranger still,
Half a dozen Englishmen helped the Rajah with a will,
Talked of noble aims and high, hinted of a future fine
For the State of Kolazai, on a strictly Western line.

Rajah Rustum held his peace; lowered octroi dues one half;
Organized a State Police; purified the Civil Staff;
Settled cess and tax afresh in a very liberal way;
Cut temptations of the flesh—also cut the Bukhshi's pay;

Roused his Secretariat to a fine Mahratta fury,
By a Hookum hinting at supervision of *dasturi;*
Turned the state of Kolazai very nearly upside-down;
When the end of May was nigh waited his achievement crown.

Then the Birthday honours came. Sad to state and sad to see,
Stood against the Rajah's name nothing more than *C. I. E.!*

. . . .

Things were lively for a week in the State of Kolazai,
Even now the people speak of that time regretfully;

How he disendowed the Gaol—stopped at once the City drain;
Turned to beauty fair and frail—got his senses back again;
Doubled taxes, cesses all; cleared away each new-built *thana;*
Turned the two-lakh Hospital into a superb Zenana;

Heaped upon the Bukhshi Sahib wealth and honours manifold;
Clad himself in Eastern garb—squeezed his people as of old.
Happy, happy Kolazai! Never more will Rustum Beg
Play to catch the Viceroy's eye. He prefers the "simpkin" peg.

The Story of Uriah

*"Now there were two men in one city;
the one rich, and the other poor."*

Jack Barrett went to Quetta
  Because they told him to.
He left his wife at Simla
  On three-fourths his monthly screw.
Jack Barrett died at Quetta
  Ere the next month's pay he drew.

Jack Barrett went to Quetta,
  He didn't understand
The reason of his transfer
  From the pleasant mountain-land;
The season was September,
  And it killed him out of hand.

Jack Barrett went to Quetta
  And there gave up the ghost:
Attempting two men's duty
  In that very healthy post;
And Mrs. Barrett mourned for him
  Five lively months at most.

Jack Barrett's bones at Quetta
  Enjoy profound repose;
But I shouldn't be astonished
  If now his spirit knows
The reason of his transfer
  From the Himalayan snows.

And, when the Last Great Bugle Call
  Adown the Hurnai throbs,
When the last grim joke is entered
  In the big black Book of Jobs,
And Quetta graveyards give again
  Their victims to the air,
I shouldn't like to be the man,
  Who sent Jack Barrett there.

My Rival

I go to concert, party, ball—
    What profit is in these?
I sit alone against the wall
    And strive to look at ease.
The incense that is mine by right
    They burn before Her shrine;
And that's because I'm seventeen
    And she is forty-nine.

I cannot check my girlish blush,
    My colour comes and goes;
I redden to my finger-tips,
    And sometimes to my nose.
But She is white where white should be
    And red where red should shine.
The blush that flies at seventeen
    Is fixed at forty-nine.

I wish *I* had Her constant cheek:
    I wish that I could sing
All sorts of funny little songs,
    Not quite the proper thing.
I'm very *gauche* and very shy,
    Her jokes aren't in my line;
And, worst of all, I'm seventeen,
    While She is forty-nine.

The young men come, the young men go,
    Each pink and white and neat,
She's older than their mothers, but
    They grovel at Her feet.
They walk beside Her 'rickshaw-wheels—
    They never walk by mine;
And that's because I'm seventeen
    And She is forty-nine.

She rides with half a dozen men
    (She calls them "boys" and "mashers")
I trot along the Mall alone;

>   My prettiest frocks and sashes
> Don't help to fill my programme-card,
>   And vainly I repine
> From ten to two A.M. Ah me!
>   Would I were forty-nine.
>
> She calls me "darling," "pet," and "dear,"
>   And "sweet retiring maid."
> I'm always at the back, I know,
>   She puts me in the shade.
> She introduces me to men,
>   "Cast" lovers, I opine,
> For sixty takes to seventeen,
>   Nineteen to forty-nine.
>
> But even She must older grow
>   And end Her dancing days,
> She can't go on for ever so
>   At concerts, balls, and plays.
> One ray of priceless hope I see
>   Before my footsteps shine:
> Just think, that She'll be eighty-one
>   When I am forty-nine!

The Betrothed

"You must choose between me and your cigar."

Open the old cigar-box, get me a Cuba stout,
For things are running crossways, and Maggie and I are out.

We quarrelled about Havanas—we fought o'er a good cheroot,
And I know she is exacting, and she says I am a brute.

Open the old cigar-box—let me consider a space;
In the soft blue veil of the vapour musing on Maggie's face.

Maggie is pretty to look at—Maggie's a loving lass,
But the prettiest cheeks must wrinkle, the truest of loves must pass.

There's peace in a Laranaga, there's calm in a Henry Clay,
But the best cigar in an hour is finished and thrown away—

Thrown away for another as perfect and ripe and brown—
But I could not throw away Maggie for fear o' the talk o' the town!

Maggie, my wife at fifty—gray and dour and old—
With never another Maggie to purchase for love or gold!

And the light of Days that have Been the dark of the Days that Are,
And Love's torch stinking and stale, like the butt of a dead cigar—

The butt of a dead cigar you are bound to keep in your pocket—
With never a new one to light tho' it's charred and black to the socket.

Open the old cigar-box—let me consider awhile—
Here is a mild Manilla—there is a wifely smile.

Which is the better portion—bondage bought with a ring,
Or a harem of dusky beauties fifty tied in a string?

Counsellors cunning and silent—comforters true and tried,
And never a one of the fifty to sneer at a rival bride.

Thought in the early morning, solace in time of woes,
Peace in the hush of the twilight, balm ere my eyelids close.

This will the fifty give me, asking naught in return,
With only a *Suttee's* passion—to do their duty and burn.

This will the fifty give me. When they are spent and dead,
Five times other fifties shall be my servants instead.

The furrows of far-off Java, the isles of the Spanish Main,
When they hear my harem is empty, will send me my brides again.

I will take no heed to their raiment, nor food for their mouths withal,
So long as the gulls are nesting, so long as the showers fall.

I will scent 'em with best Vanilla, with tea will I temper their hides,
And the Moor and the Mormon shall envy who read of the tale of my brides.

For Maggie has written a letter that gives me my choice between
The wee little whimpering Love and the great god Nick o' Teen.

And I have been servant of Love for barely a twelve-month clear,
But I have been Priest of Partagas a matter of seven year;

And the gloom of my bachelor days is flecked with the cheery light
Of stumps that I burned to Friendship and Pleasure and Work and Fight.

And I turn my eyes to the future that Maggie and I must prove,
But the only light on the marshes is the Will-o'-the-Wisp of Love.

Will it see me safe through my journey or leave me bogged in the mire?
Since a puff of tobacco can cloud it, shall I follow the fitful fire?

Open the old cigar-box—let me consider anew—
Old friends, and who is Maggie that I should abandon *you*?

A million surplus Maggies are willing to bear the yoke;
And a woman is only a woman, but a good cigar is a Smoke.

Light me another Cuba—I hold to my first-sworn vows,
If Maggie will have no rival, I'll have no Maggie for spouse!

The Ballad of East and West

Oh, East is East, and West is West, and never the twain shall meet,
Till Earth and Sky stand presently at God's great Judgment Seat;
But there is neither East nor West, Border, nor Breed, nor Birth,
When two strong men stand face to face, tho' they come from the ends of the earth!

Kamal is out with twenty men to raise the Border side,
And he has lifted the Colonel's mare that is the Colonel's pride:
He has lifted her out of the stable-door between the dawn and the day,
And turned the calkins upon her feet, and ridden her far away.
Then up and spoke the Colonel's son that led a troop of the Guides:
'Is there never a man of all my men can say where Kamal hides?'
Then up and spoke Mahommed Khan, the son of the Ressaldar,
'If ye know the track of the morning-mist, ye know where his pickets are.
'At dusk he harries the Abazai—at dawn he is into Bonair,
'But he must go by Fort Bukloh to his own place to fare,
'So if ye gallop to Fort Bukloh as fast as a bird can fly,
'By the favour of God ye may cut him off ere he win to the Tongue of Jagai,
'But if he be passed the Tongue of Jagai, right swiftly turn ye then,
'For the length and the breadth of that grisly plain is sown with Kamal's men.
'There is rock to the left, and rock to the right, and low lean thorn between,
'And ye may hear a breech-bolt snick where never a man is seen.'

The Colonel's son has taken a horse, and a raw rough dun was he,
With the mouth of a bell and the heart of Hell, and the head of the gallows-tree.
The Colonel's son to the Fort has won, they bid him stay to eat—
Who rides at the tail of a Border thief, he sits not long at his meat.
He's up and away from Fort Bukloh as fast as he can fly,
Till he was aware of his father's mare in the gut of the Tongue of Jagai,
Till he was aware of his father's mare with Kamal upon her back,
And when he could spy the white of her eye, he made the pistol crack.
He has fired once, he has fired twice, but the whistling ball went wide.
'Ye shoot like a soldier,' Kamal said. 'Show now if ye can ride.'
It's up and over the Tongue of Jagai, as blown dust-devils go,
The dun he fled like a stag of ten, but the mare like a barren doe.
The dun he leaned against the bit and slugged his head above,
But the red mare played with the snaffle-bars, as a maiden plays with a glove.
There was rock to the left and rock to the right, and low lean thorn between,
And thrice he heard a breech-bolt snick tho' never a man was seen.
They have ridden the low moon out of the sky, their hoofs drum up the dawn,
The dun he went like a wounded bull, but the mare like a new-roused fawn.
The dun he fell at a water-course—in a woful heap fell he,
And Kamal has turned the red mare back, and pulled the rider free.
He has knocked the pistol out of his hand—small room was there to strive,
' 'Twas only by favour of mine,' quoth he, 'ye rode so long alive:
'There was not a rock for twenty mile, there was not a clump of tree,
'But covered a man of my own men with his rifle cocked on his knee.
'If I had raised my bridle-hand, as I have held it low,
'The little jackals that flee so fast, were feasting all in a row:
'If I had bowed my head on my breast, as I have held it high,
'The kite that whistles above us now were gorged till she could not fly.'
Lightly answered the Colonel's son:—'Do good to bird and beast,
'But count who come for the broken meats before thou makest a feast.
'If there should follow a thousand swords to carry my bones away,

'Belike the price of a jackal's meal were more than a thief could pay.
'They will feed their horse on the standing crop, their men on the
　　garnered grain,
'The thatch of the byres will serve their fires when all the cattle are
　　slain.
'But if thou thinkest the price be fair,—thy brethren wait to sup,
'The hound is kin to the jackal-spawn,—howl, dog, and call them
　　up!
'And if thou thinkest the price be high, in steer and gear and stack,
'Give me my father's mare again, and I'll fight my own way back!'
Kamal has gripped him by the hand and set him upon his feet.
'No talk shall be of dogs,' said he, 'when wolf and grey wolf meet.
'May I eat dirt if thou hast hurt of me in deed or breath;
'What dam of lances brought thee forth to jest at the dawn with
　　Death?'
Lightly answered the Colonel's son: 'I hold by the blood of my clan:
'Take up the mare for my father's gift—by God, she has carried a
　　man!'
The red mare ran to the Colonel's son, and nuzzled against his
　　breast,
'We be two strong men,' said Kamal then, 'but she loveth the younger
　　best.
'So she shall go with a lifter's dower, my turquoise-studded rein,
'My broidered saddle and saddle-cloth, and silver stirrups twain.'
The Colonel's son a pistol drew and held it muzzle-end,
'Ye have taken the one from a foe,' said he; 'will ye take the mate
　　from a friend?'
'A gift for a gift,' said Kamal straight; 'a limb for the risk of a limb.
'Thy father has sent his son to me, I'll send my son to him!'
With that he whistled his only son, that dropped from a mountain-
　　crest—
He trod the ling like a buck in spring, and he looked like a lance in
　　rest.
'Now here is thy master,' Kamal said, 'who leads a troop of the
　　Guides,
'And thou must ride at his left side as shield on shoulder rides.
'Till Death or I cut loose the tie, at camp and board and bed,
'Thy life is his—thy fate it is to guard him with thy head.
'So thou must eat the White Queen's meat, and all her foes are thine,
'And thou must harry thy father's hold for the peace of the Border-
　　line,
'And thou must make a trooper tough and hack thy way to power—

'Belike they will raise thee to Ressaldar when I am hanged in
  Peshawur.'

They have looked each other between the eyes, and there they found
  no fault,
They have taken the Oath of the Brother-in-Blood on leavened bread
  and salt:
They have taken the Oath of the Brother-in-Blood on fire and fresh-
  cut sod,
On the hilt and the haft of the Khyber knife, and the Wondrous
  Names of God.
The Colonel's son he rides the mare and Kamal's boy the dun,
And two have come back to Fort Bukloh where there went forth but
  one.
And when they drew to the Quarter-Guard, full twenty swords flew
  clear—
There was not a man but carried his feud with the blood of the
  mountaineer.
'Ha' done! ha' done!' said the Colonel's son. 'Put up the steel at your
  sides!
Last night ye had struck at a Border thief—tonight 'tis a man of the
  Guides!'

Oh, East is East, and West is West, and never the two shall meet,
Till Earth and Sky stand presently at God's great Judgment Seat;
But there is neither East nor West, Border, nor Breed, nor Birth,
When two strong men stand face to face, tho' they come from the ends
  of the earth.

The Ballad of the King's Mercy

Abdhur Rahman, the Durani Chief, of him is the story told.
His mercy fills the Khyber hills—his grace is manifold;
He has taken toll of the North and the South—his glory reacheth
  far,
And they tell the tale of his charity from Balkh to Kandahar.

Before the old Peshawur Gate, where Kurd and Kaffir meet,
The Governor of Kabul dealt the Justice of the Street,
And that was strait as running noose and swift as plunging knife,
Tho' he who held the longer purse might hold the longer life.
There was a hound of Hindustan had struck a Euzufzai,

Wherefore they spat upon his face and led him out to die.
It chanced the King went forth that hour when throat was bared to
  knife;
The Kaffir grovelled under-hoof and clamoured for his life.

Then said the King: 'Have hope, O friend! Yea, Death disgraced is
  hard;
'Much honour shall be thine'; and called the Captain of the Guard,
Yar Khan, a bastard of the Blood, so city-babble saith,
And he was honoured of the King—the which is salt to Death;
And he was son of Daoud Shah the Reiver of the Plains,
And blood of old Durani Lords ran fire in his veins;
And 'twas to tame an Afghan pride nor Hell nor Heaven could bind,
The King would make him butcher to a yelping cur of Hind.
'Strike!' said the King. 'King's blood art thou—his death shall be his
  pride!'
Then louder, that the crowd might catch: 'Fear not—his arms are
  tied!'
Yar Khan drew clear the Khyber knife, and struck, and sheathed
  again.
'O man, thy will is done,' quoth he; 'A King this dog hath slain.'

> Abdhur Rahman, the Durani Chief, to the North and the South is
>   sold.
> The North and the South shall open their mouth to a Ghilzai flag
>   unrolled,
> When the big guns speak to the Khyber peak, and his dog-Heratis
>   fly,
> Ye have heard the song—How long? How long? Wolves of the
>   Abazai!

That night before the watch was set, when all the streets were clear,
The Governor of Kabul spoke: 'My King, hast thou no fear?
'Thou knowest—thou hast heard,'—his speech died at his master's
  face.
And grimly said the Afghan King: 'I rule the Afghan race.
'My path is mine—see thou to thine—to-night upon thy bed
'Think who there be in Kabul now that clamour for thy head.'

That night when all the gates were shut to City and to Throne,
Within a little garden-house the King lay down alone.
Before the sinking of the moon, which is the Night of Night,
 Yar Khan came softly to the King to make his honour white.
 The children of the town had mocked beneath his horse's hoofs,

The harlots of the town had hailed him 'butcher!' from their roofs.
But as he groped against the wall, two hands upon him fell,
The King behind his shoulder spoke: 'Dead man, thou dost not well!
' 'Tis ill to jest with Kings by day and seek a boon by night;
'And that thou bearest in thy hand is all too sharp to write.
'But three days hence, if God be good, and if thy strength remain,
'Thou shalt demand one boon of me and bless me in thy pain.
'For I am merciful to all, and most of all to thee.
'My butcher of the shambles, rest—no knife hast thou for me!'

> Abdhur Rahman, the Durani Chief, holds hard by the South and the North;
> But the Ghilzai knows, ere the melting snows, when the swollen banks break forth,
> When the red-coats crawl to the sungar wall, and his Usbeg lances fail.
> Ye have heard the song—How long? How long? Wolves of the Zuka Kheyl!

They stoned him in the rubbish-field when dawn was in the sky,
According to the written word, 'See that he do not die.'
They stoned him till the stones were piled above him on the plain,
And those the labouring limbs displaced they tumbled back again.

One watched beside the dreary mound that veiled the battered thing,
And him the King with laughter called the Herald of the King.

It was upon the second night, the night of Ramazan,
The watcher leaning earthward heard the message of Yar Khan.
From shattered breast through shrivelled lips broke forth the rattling breath:
'Creature of God, deliver me from agony of Death.'

They sought the King among his girls, and risked their lives thereby:
'Protector of the Pitiful, give orders that he die!'

'Bid him endure until the day,' a lagging answer came;
'The night is short, and he can pray and learn to bless my name.'

Before the dawn three times he spoke, and on the day once more:
'Creature of God, deliver me and bless the King therefore!'

They shot him at the morning prayer, to ease him of his pain,
And when he heard the matchlocks clink, he blessed the King again.

Which thing the singers made a song for all the world to sing,
So that the Outer Seas may know the mercy of the King.

> Abdhur Rahman, the Durani Chief, of him is the story told.
> He has opened his mouth to the North and the South, they have
>   stuffed his mouth with gold.
> Ye know the truth of his tender ruth—and sweet his favours are.
> Ye have heard the song—How long? How long? from Balkh to
>   Kandahar.

The Ballad of the 'Bolivar'

> Seven men from all the world, back to Docks again,
> Rolling down the Ratcliffe Road drunk and raising Cain:
> Give the girls another drink 'fore we sign away—
> We that took the 'Bolivar' out across the Bay!

We put out from Sunderland loaded down with rails;
   We put back to Sunderland 'cause our cargo shifted;
We put out from Sunderland—met the winter gales—
   Seven days and seven nights to the Start we drifted.

> Racketing her rivets loose, smoke-stack white as snow,
> All the coals adrift a deck, half the rails below
> Leaking like a lobster-pot, steering like a dray—
> Out we took the 'Bolivar,' out across the Bay!

One by one the Lights came up, winked and let us by;
   Mile by mile we waddled on, coal and fo'c'sle short;
Met a blow that laid us down, heard a bulkhead fly;
   Left The Wolf behind us with a two-foot list to port.

> Trailing like a wounded duck, working out her soul;
> Clanging like a smithy-shop after every roll;
> Just a funnel and a mast lurching through the spray—
> So we threshed the 'Bolivar' out across the Bay!

Felt her hog and felt her sag, betted when she'd break;
   Wondered every time she raced if she'd stand the shock;
Heard the seas like drunken men pounding at her strake;
   Hoped the Lord 'ud keep his thumb on the plummer-block.

>   Banged against the iron decks, bilges choked with coal;
>   Flayed and frozen foot and hand, sick of heart and soul;
>   'Last we prayed she'd buck herself into Judgment Day—
>   Hi! we cursed the 'Bolivar' knocking round the Bay!

Oh! her nose flung up to sky, groaning to be still—
>   Up and down and back we went, never time for breath;
Then the money paid at Lloyd's caught her by the heel,
>   And the stars ran round and round dancin' at our death.

>   Aching for an hour's sleep, dozing off between;
>   Heard the rotten rivets draw when she took it green;
>   Watched the compass chase its tail like a cat at play—
>   That was on the 'Bolivar,' south across the Bay.

Once we saw between the squalls, lyin' head to swell—
>   Mad with work and weariness, wishin' they was we—
Some damned Liner's lights go by like a grand hotel;
>   Cheered her from the 'Bolivar,' swampin' in the sea.

>   Then a greyback cleared us out, then the skipper laughed;
>   'Boys, the wheel has gone to Hell—rig the winches aft!
>   'Yoke the kicking rudder-head—get her under way!'
>   So we steered her, pulley-haul, out across the Bay!

Just a pack o' rotten plates puttied up with tar,
>   In we came, an' time enough 'cross Bilbao Bar.
>   Overloaded, undermanned, meant to founder, we
>   Euchred God Almighty's storm, bluffed the Eternal Sea!

>   *Seven men from all the world, back to town again,*
>   *Rollin' down the Ratcliffe Road drunk and raising Cain:*
>   *Seven men from out of Hell. Ain't the owners gay,*
>   *'Cause we took the 'Bolivar' safe across the Bay?*

The Conundrum of the Workshops

When the flush of a new-born sun fell first on Eden's green and gold,
Our father Adam sat under the Tree and scratched with a stick in the mould;

And the first rude sketch that the world had seen was joy to his
  mighty heart,
Till the Devil whispered behind the leaves, 'It's pretty, but is it Art?'

Wherefore he called to his wife, and fled to fashion his work anew—
The first of his race who cared a fig for the first, most dread review;
And he left his lore to the use of his sons—and that was a glorious
  gain
When the Devil chuckled 'Is it Art?' in the ear of the branded Cain.

They built a tower to shiver the sky and wrench the stars apart,
Till the Devil grunted behind the bricks: 'It's striking, but is it Art?'
The stone was dropped at the quarry-side and the idle derrick
  swung,
While each man talked of the aims of Art, and each in an alien
  tongue.

They fought and they talked in the North and the South, they talked
  and they fought in the West,
Till the waters rose on the pitiful land, and the poor Red Clay had
  rest—
Had rest till the dank, blank-canvas dawn when the dove was
  preened to start,
And the Devil bubbled below the keel: 'It's human, but is it Art?'

The tale is as old as the Eden Tree—and new as the new-cut tooth—
For each man knows ere his lip-thatch grows he is master of Art and
  Truth;
And each man hears as the twilight nears, to the beat of his dying
  heart,
The Devil drum on the darkened pane: 'You did it, but was it Art?'

We have learned to whittle the Eden Tree to the shape of a surplice-
  peg,
We have learned to bottle our parents twain in the yelk of an addled
  egg,
We know that the tail must wag the dog, for the horse is drawn by the
  cart;
But the Devil whoops, as he whooped of old: 'It's clever, but is it
  Art?'

When the flicker of London sun falls faint on the Club-room's green
  and gold,
The sons of Adam sit them down and scratch with their pens in the
  mould—

They scratch with their pens in the mould of their graves, and the ink
    and the anguish start,
For the Devil mutters behind the leaves: 'It's pretty, but is it Art?'

Now, if we could win to the Eden Tree where the Four Great Rivers
    flow,
And the Wreath of Eve is red on the turf as she left it long ago,
And if we could come when the sentry slept and softly scurry
    through,
By the favour of God we might know as much—as our father Adam
    knew.

In the Neolithic Age

In the Neolithic Age savage warfare did I wage
    For food and fame and two-toed horses' pelt;
I was singer to my clan in that dim, red Dawn of Man,
    And I sang of all we fought and feared and felt.

Yea, I sang as now I sing, when the Prehistoric spring
    Made the piled Biscayan ice-pack split and shove,
And the troll and gnome and dwerg, and the Gods of Cliff and Berg
    Were about me and beneath me and above.

But a rival of Solutré told the tribe my style was *outré*—
    By a hammer, grooved of dolomite, he fell.
And I left my views on Art, barbed and tanged, beneath the heart
    Of a mammothistic etcher at Grenelle.

Then I stripped them, scalp from skull, and my hunting dogs fed
    full,
    And their teeth I threaded neatly on a thong;
And I wiped my mouth and said, "It is well that they are dead,
    For I know my work is right and theirs was wrong."

But my Totem saw the shame; from his ridgepole shrine he came,
    And he told me in a vision of the night:—
"There are nine and sixty ways of constructing tribal lays,
    And every single one of them is right!"

    .   .   .   .

Then the silence closed upon me till They put new clothing on me
    Of whiter, weaker flesh and bone more frail;

And I stepped beneath Time's finger once again a tribal singer
    And a minor poet certified by Tr—l.

Still they skirmish to and fro, men my messmates on the snow,
    When we headed off the aurochs turn for turn;
When the rich Allobrogenses never kept amanuenses,
    And our only plots were piled in lakes at Berne.

Still a cultured Christian age sees us scuffle, squeak, and rage,
    Still we pinch and slap and jabber—scratch and dirk;
Still we let our business slide—as we dropped the half-dressed hide—
To show a fellow-savage how to work.

Still the world is wondrous large,—seven seas from marge to marge,—
    And it holds a vast of various kinds of man;
And the wildest dreams of Kew are the facts of Khatmandhu
    And the crimes of Clapham chaste in Martaban.

Here's my wisdom for your use, as I learned it when the moose
    And the reindeer roared where Paris roars to-night:
There are nine and sixty ways of constructing tribal lays,
    And—every—single—one—of—them—is—right.

The English Flag

> *Above the portico a flag-staff, bearing the Union Jack, remained fluttering in the flames for some time, but ultimately when it fell the crowds rent the air with shouts, and seemed to see significance in the incident.*—DAILY PAPERS.

Winds of the World, give answer? They are whimpering to and fro—
And what should they know of England who only England know?—
The poor little street-bred people that vapour and fume and brag,
They are lifting their heads in the stillness to yelp at the English Flag!

Must we borrow a clout from the Boer—to plaster anew with dirt?
An Irish liar's bandage, or an English coward's shirt?
We may not speak of England; her Flag's to sell or share.
What is the Flag of England? Winds of the World, declare!

The North Wind blew:—'From Bergen my steel-shod van-guards go;
'I chase your lazy whalers home from the Disko floe;
'By the great North Lights above me I work the will of God,
'That the liner splits on the ice-field or the Dogger fills with cod.

'I barred my gates with iron, I shuttered my doors with flame,
'Because to force my ramparts your nutshell navies came;
'I took the sun from their presence, I cut them down with my blast,
'And they died, but the Flag of England blew free ere the spirit passed.

'The lean white bear hath seen it in the long, long Arctic night,
'The musk-ox knows the standard that flouts the Northern Light:
'What is the Flag of England? Ye have but my bergs to dare,
'Ye have but my drifts to conquer. Go forth, for it is there!'

The South Wind sighed:—'From The Virgins my mid-sea course was ta'en
'Over a thousand islands lost in an idle main,
'Where the sea-egg flames on the coral and the long-backed breakers croon
'Their endless ocean legends to the lazy, locked lagoon.

'Strayed amid lonely islets, mazed amid outer keys,
'I waked the palms to laughter—I tossed the scud in the breeze—
'Never was isle so little, never was sea so lone,
'But over the scud and the palm-trees an English flag was flown.

'I have wrenched it free from the halliard to hang for a wisp on the Horn;
'I have chased it north to the Lizard—ribboned and rolled and torn;
'I have spread its fold o'er the dying, adrift in a hopeless sea;
'I have hurled it swift on the slaver, and seen the slave set free.

'My basking sunfish know it, and wheeling albatross,
'Where the lone wave fills with fire beneath the Southern Cross.
'What is the Flag of England? Ye have but my reefs to dare,
'Ye have but my seas to furrow. Go forth, for it is there!'

The East Wind roared:—'From the Kuriles, the Bitter Seas, I come,
'And me men call the Home-Wind, for I bring the English home.
'Look—look well to your shipping! By the breath of my mad typhoon
'I swept your close-packed Praya and beached your best at Kowloon!

'The reeling junks behind me and the racing seas before,
'I raped your richest roadstead—I plundered Singapore!

'I set my hand on the Hoogli; as a hooded snake she rose,
'And I flung your stoutest steamers to roost with the startled crows.

'Never the lotos closes, never the wild-fowl wake,
'But a soul goes out on the East Wind that died for England's sake—
'Man or woman or suckling, mother or bride or maid—
'Because on the bones of the English the English Flag is stayed.

'The desert-dust hath dimmed it, the flying wild-ass knows
'The scared white leopard winds it across the taintless snows.
'What is the Flag of England? Ye have but my sun to dare,
'Ye have but my sands to travel. Go forth, for it is there!'

The West Wind called:—'In squadrons the thoughtless galleons fly
'That bear the wheat and cattle lest street-bred people die.
'They make my might their porter, they make my house their path,
'Till I loose my neck from their rudder and whelm them all in my wrath.

'I draw the gliding fog-bank as a snake is drawn from the hole;
'They bellow one to the other, the frighted ship-bells toll,
'For day is a drifting terror till I raise the shroud with my breath,
'And they see strange bows above them and the two go locked to death.

'But whether in calm or wrack-wreath, whether by dark or day,
'I heave them whole to the conger or rip their plates away,
'First of the scattered legions, under a shrieking sky,
'Dipping between the rollers, the English Flag goes by.

'The dead dumb fog hath wrapped it—the frozen dews have kissed—
'The naked stars have seen it, a fellow-star in the mist.
'What is the Flag of England? Ye have but my breath to dare,
'Ye have but my waves to conquer. Go forth, for it is there!'

Tomlinson

Now Tomlinson gave up the ghost in his house in Berkeley Square,
And a Spirit came to his bedside and gripped him by the hair—
A Spirit gripped him by the hair and carried him far away,
Till he heard as the roar of a rain-fed ford the roar of the Milky Way,

Till he heard the roar of the Milky Way die down and drone and
    cease,
And they came to the Gate within the Wall where Peter holds the
    keys.
'Stand up, stand up now, Tomlinson, and answer loud and high
'The good that ye did for the sake of men or ever ye came to die—
'The good that ye did for the sake of men in little earth so lone!'
And the naked soul of Tomlinson grew white as a rain-washed bone.
'O, I have a friend on earth,' he said, 'that was my priest and guide,
'And well would he answer all for me if he were by my side.'
—'For that ye strove in neighbour-love it shall be written fair,
'But now ye wait at Heaven's Gate and not in Berkeley Square:
'Though we called your friend from his bed this night, he could not
    speak for you,
'For the race is run by one and one and never by two and two.'
Then Tomlinson looked up and down, and little gain was there,
For the naked stars grinned overhead, and he saw that his soul was
    bare:
The Wind that blows between the worlds, it cut him like a knife,
And Tomlinson took up his tale and spoke of his good in life.
'This I have read in a book,' he said, 'and that was told to me,
'And this I have thought that another man thought of a Prince in
    Muscovy.'
The good souls flocked like homing doves and bade him clear the
    path,
And Peter twirled the jangling keys in weariness and wrath.
'Ye have read, ye have heard, ye have thought,' he said, 'and the tale
    is yet to run:
'By the worth of the body that once ye had, give answer—what ha' ye
    done?'
Then Tomlinson looked back and forth, and little good it bore,
For the Darkness stayed at his shoulder-blade and Heaven's Gate
    before:
'Oh, this I have felt, and this I have guessed, and this I have heard
    men say,
'And this they wrote that another man wrote of a carl in Norroway.'
'Ye have read, ye have felt, ye have guessed, good lack! Ye have
    hampered Heaven's Gate;
'There's little room between the stars in idleness to prate!
'Oh, none may reach by hired speech of neighbour, priest, and kin,
'Through borrowed deed to God's good meed that lies so fair within;
'Get hence, get hence to the Lord of Wrong, for doom has yet to run,

'And . . . the faith that ye share with Berkeley Square uphold you,
   Tomlinson!'

. . . .

The Spirit gripped him by the hair, and sun by sun they fell
Till they came to the belt of Naughty Stars that rim the mouth of Hell:
The first are red with pride and wrath, the next are white with pain,
But the third are black with clinkered sin that cannot burn again:
They may hold their path, they may leave their path, with never a
   soul to mark,
They may burn or freeze, but they must not cease in the Scorn of the
   Outer Dark.
The Wind that blows between the worlds, it nipped him to the bone,
And he yearned to the flare of Hell-gate there as the light of his own
   hearth-stone.
The Devil he sat behind the bars, where the desperate legions drew,
But he caught the hasting Tomlinson and would not let him through.
'Wot ye the price of good pit-coal that I must pay?' said he,
'That ye rank yoursel' so fit for Hell and ask no leave of me?
'I am all o'er-sib to Adam's breed that ye should give me scorn,
'For I strove with God for your First Father the day that he was born.
'Sit down, sit down upon the slag, and answer loud and high
'The harm that ye did to the Sons of Men or ever you came to die.'
And Tomlinson looked up and up, and saw against the night
The belly of a tortured star blood-red in Hell-Mouth light;
And Tomlinson looked down and down, and saw beneath his feet
The frontlet of a tortured star milk-white in Hell-Mouth heat.
'Oh, I had a love on earth,' said he, 'that kissed me to my fall,
'And if ye would call my love to me I know she would answer all.'
—'All that ye did in love forbid it shall be written fair,
'But now ye wait at Hell-Mouth Gate and not in Berkeley Square:
'Though we whistled your love from her bed to-night, I trow she
   would not run,
'For the sin ye do by two and two ye must pay for one by one!'
The Wind that blows between the worlds, it cut him like a knife,
And Tomlinson took up the tale and spoke of his sin in life:
'Once I ha' laughed at the power of Love and twice at the grip of the
   Grave,
'And thrice I ha' patted my God on the head that men might call me
   brave.'
The Devil he blew on a brandered soul and set it aside to cool:

'Do ye think I would waste my good pit-coal on the hide of a brain-sick fool?
'I see no worth in the hobnailed mirth or the jolt-head jest ye did
'That I should waken my gentlemen that are sleeping three on a grid.'
Then Tomlinson looked back and forth, and there was little grace,
For Hell-Gate filled the houseless Soul with the Fear of Naked Space.
'Nay, this I ha' heard,' quo' Tomlinson, 'and this was noised abroad,
'And this I ha' got from a Belgian book on the word of a dead French lord.'
—'Ye ha' heard, ye ha' read, ye ha' got, good lack! And the tale begins afresh—
'Have ye sinned one sin for the pride o' the eye or the sinful lust of the flesh?'
Then Tomlinson he gripped the bars and yammered 'Let me in—
'For I mind that I borrowed my neighbour's wife to sin the deadly sin.'
The Devil he grinned behind the bars, and banked the fires high:
'Did ye read of that sin in a book?' said he; and Tomlinson said 'Ay!'
The Devil he blew upon his nails, and the little devils ran;
And he said, 'Go husk this whimpering thief that comes in the guise of a man:
'Winnow him out 'twixt star and star, and sieve his proper worth:
'There's sore decline in Adam's line if this be spawn of earth.'
Empusa's crew, so naked-new they may not face the fire,
But weep that they bin too small to sin to the height of their desire,
Over the coal they chased the Soul, and racked it all abroad,
As children rifle a caddis-case or the raven's foolish hoard.
And back they came with the tattered Thing, as children after play,
And they said: 'The soul that he got from God he has bartered clean away.
'We have threshed a stook of print and book, and winnowed a chattering wind
'And many a soul wherefrom he stole, but his we cannot find:
'We have handled him, we have dandled him, we have seared him to the bone,
'And sure if tooth and nail show truth he has no soul of his own.'
The Devil he bowed his head on his breast and rumbled deep and low:—
'I'm all o'er-sib to Adam's breed that I should bid him go.

'Yet close we lie, and deep we lie, and if I gave him place,
'My gentlemen that are so proud would flout me to my face;
'They'd call my house a common stews and me a careless host,
'And—I would not anger my gentlemen for the sake of a shiftless ghost.'
The Devil he looked at the mangled Soul that prayed to feel the flame,
And he thought of Holy Charity, but he thought of his own good name:
'Now ye could haste my coal to waste, and sit ye down to fry:
'Did ye think of that theft for yourself?' said he; and Tomlinson said 'Ay!'
The Devil he blew an outward breath, for his heart was free from care:
'Ye have scarce the soul of a louse,' he said, 'but the roots of sin are there,
'And for that sin should ye come in were I the lord alone.
'But sinful pride has rule inside—and mightier than my own.
'Honour and Wit, fore-damned they sit, to each his priest and whore:
'Nay, scarce I dare myself go there, and you they'd torture sore.
'Ye are neither spirit nor spirk,' he said; 'ye are neither book nor brute—
'Go, get ye back to the flesh again for the sake of Man's repute.
'I'm all o'er-sib to Adam's breed that I should mock your pain,
'But look that ye win to worthier sin ere ye come back again.
'Get hence, the hearse is at your door—the grim black stallions wait—
'They bear your clay to place to-day. Speed, lest ye come too late!
'Go back to Earth with a lip unsealed—go back with an open eye,
'And carry my word to the Sons of Men or ever ye come to die:
'That the sin they do by two and two they must pay for one by one—
'And . . . the God that you took from a printed book be with you, Tomlinson!'

Danny Deever

'What are the bugles blowin' for?' said Files-on-Parade.
'To turn you out, to turn you out,' the Colour-Sergeant said.
'What makes you look so white, so white?' said Files-on-Parade.
'I'm dreadin' what I've got to watch,' the Colour-Sergeant said.

  For they're hangin' Danny Deever, you can hear the Dead
   March play,
  The regiment's in 'ollow square—they're hangin' him to-
   day;
  They've taken of his buttons off an' cut his stripes away,
  An' they're hangin' Danny Deever in the mornin'.

'What makes the rear-rank breathe so 'ard?' said Files-on-Parade.
'It's bitter cold, it's bitter cold,' the Colour-Sergeant said.
'What makes that front-rank man fall down?' says Files-on-Parade.
'A touch o' sun, a touch o' sun,' the Colour-Sergeant said.

  They are hangin' Danny Deever, they are marchin' of 'im
   round,
  They 'ave 'alted Danny Deever by 'is coffin on the ground;
  An' 'e'll swing in 'arf a minute for a sneakin' shootin'
   hound—
  O they're hangin' Danny Deever in the mornin'!

' 'Is cot was right-'and cot to mine,' said Files-on-Parade.
' 'E's sleepin' out an' far to-night,' the Colour-Sergeant said.
'I've drunk 'is beer a score o' times,' said Files-on-Parade.
' 'E's drinkin' bitter beer alone,' the Colour-Sergeant said.

  They are hangin' Danny Deever, you must mark 'im to 'is
   place,
  For 'e shot a comrade sleepin'—you must look 'im in the
   face;
  Nine 'undred of 'is county an' the regiment's disgrace,
  While they're hangin' Danny Deever in the mornin'.

'What's that so black agin the sun?' said Files-on-Parade.
'It's Danny fightin' 'ard for life,' the Colour-Sergeant said.
'What's that that whimpers over'ead?' said Files-on-Parade.
'It's Danny's soul that's passin' now,' the Colour-Sergeant said.

  For they're done with Danny Deever, you can 'ear the quick-
   step play,
  The regiment's in column, an' they're marchin' us away;
  Ho! the young recruits are shakin', an' they'll want their beer
   to-day,
  After hangin' Danny Deever in the mornin'.

Tommy

I went into a public-'ouse to get a pint o' beer,
The publican 'e up an' sez, 'We serve no red-coats here.'
The girls be'ind the bar they laughed an' giggled fit to die,
I outs into the street again an' to myself sez I:

> O it's Tommy this, an' Tommy that, an' 'Tommy, go away';
> But it's 'Thank you, Mister Atkins,' when the band begins to play,
> The band begins to play, my boys, the band begins to play.
> O it's 'Thank you, Mister Atkins,' when the band begins to play.

I went into a theatre as sober as could be,
They gave a drunk civilian room, but 'adn't none for me;
They sent me to the gallery or round the music-'alls,
But when it comes to fightin', Lord! they'll shove me in the stalls!

> For it's Tommy this, an' Tommy that, an' 'Tommy, wait outside';
> But it's 'Special train for Atkins' when the trooper's on the tide,
> The troopship's on the tide, my boys, the troopship's on the tide,
> O it's 'Special train for Atkins' when the trooper's on the tide.

Yes, makin' mock o' uniforms that guard you while you sleep
Is cheaper than them uniforms, an' they're starvation cheap;
An' hustlin' drunken soldiers when they're goin' large a bit
Is five times better business than paradin' in full kit.

> Then it's Tommy this, an' Tommy that, an' 'Tommy, 'ow's yer soul?'
> But it's 'Thin red line of 'eroes' when the drums begin to roll,
> The drums begin to roll, my boys, the drums begin to roll,
> O it's 'Thin red line of 'eroes' when the drums begin to roll.

We aren't no thin red 'eroes, nor we aren't no blackguards too,
But single men in barricks, most remarkable like you;
An' if sometimes our conduck isn't all your fancy paints:
Why, single men in barricks don't grow into plaster saints;

> While it's Tommy this, an' Tommy that, an' 'Tommy, fall be'ind,'

> But it's 'Please to walk in front, sir,' when there's trouble in
> the wind,
> There's trouble in the wind, my boys, there's trouble in the
> wind,
> O it's 'Please to walk in front, sir,' when there's trouble in the
> wind.

You talk o' better food for us, an' schools, an' fires, an' all:
We'll wait for extry rations if you treat us rational.
Don't mess about the cook-room slops, but prove it to our face
The Widow's Uniform is not the soldier-man's disgrace.

> For it's Tommy this, an' Tommy that, an' 'Chuck him out, the
> brute!'
> But it's 'Saviour of 'is country,' when the guns begin to shoot;
> Yes it's Tommy this, an' Tommy that, an' anything you please;
> But Tommy ain't a bloomin' fool—you bet that Tommy sees!

'Fuzzy-Wuzzy'

(SOUDAN EXPEDITIONARY FORCE)

We've fought with many men acrost the seas,
   An' some of 'em was brave an' some was not
The Paythan an' the Zulu an' Burmese;
   But the Fuzzy was the finest o' the lot.
We never got a ha'porth's change of 'im:
   'E squatted in the scrub an' 'ocked our 'orses,
'E cut our sentries up at Sua*kim*,
   An' 'e played the cat an' banjo with our forces.

> So 'ere's *to* you, Fuzzy-Wuzzy, at your 'ome in the Soudan;
> You're a pore benighted 'eathen but a first-class fightin' man;
> We gives you your certificate, an' if you want it signed
> We'll come an' 'ave a romp with you whenever you're in-
> clined.

We took our chanst among the Kyber 'ills,
   The Boers knocked us silly at a mile,
The Burman give us Irriwaddy chills,
   An' a Zulu *impi* dished us up in style:

But all we ever got from such as they
    Was pop to what the Fuzzy made us swaller;
We 'eld our bloomin' own, the papers say,
    But man for man the Fuzzy knocked us 'oller.

> Then 'ere's *to* you, Fuzzy-Wuzzy, an' the missis and the kid;
> Our orders was to break you, an' of course we went an' did.
> We sloshed you with Martinis, an' it wasn't 'ardly fair;
>   But for all the odds agin' you, Fuzzy-Wuz you broke the square.

'E 'asn't got no papers of 'is own,
    'E 'asn't got no medals nor rewards,
So we must certify the skill 'e's shown
    In usin' of 'is long two-'anded swords:
When 'e's 'oppin' in an' out among the bush
    With 'is coffin-'eaded shield an' shovel-spear,
An 'appy day with Fuzzy on the rush
    Will last an 'ealthy Tommy for a year.

> So 'ere's *to* you, Fuzzy-Wuzzy, an' your friends which are no more,
> If we 'adn't lost some messmates we would 'elp you to deplore;
> But give an' take's the gospel, an' we'll call the bargain fair,
>   For if you 'ave lost more than us, you crumpled up the square!

'E rushes at the smoke when we let drive,
    An', before we know, 'e's 'ackin' at our 'ead;
'E's all 'ot sand an' ginger when alive,
    An' 'e's generally shammin' when 'e's dead.
'E's a daisy, 'e's a ducky, 'e's a lamb!
    'E's a injia-rubber idiot on the spree,
'E's the on'y thing that doesn't give a damn
    For a Regiment o' British Infantree!

> So 'ere's *to* you, Fuzzy-Wuzzy, at your 'ome in the Soudan;
> You're a pore benighted 'eathen but a first-class fightin' man;
> An' 'ere's *to* you, Fuzzy-Wuzzy, with your 'ayrick 'ead of 'air—
>   You big black boundin' beggar—for you broke a British square!

Gunga Din

You may talk o' gin and beer
When you're quartered safe out 'ere,
An' you're sent to penny-fights an' Aldershot it;
But when it comes to slaughter
You will do your work on water,
An' you'll lick the bloomin' boots of 'im that's got it.
Now in Injia's sunny clime,
Where I used to spend my time
A-servin' of 'Er Majesty the Queen,
Of all them blackfaced crew
The finest man I knew
Was our regimental bhisti, Gunga Din.
    He was 'Din! Din! Din!
    You limping lump o' brick-dust, Gunga Din!
    Hi! slippery hitherao!
    Water, get it! Panee lao![1]
    You squidgy-nosed old idol, Gunga Din.'

The uniform 'e wore
Was nothin' much before,
An' rather less than 'arf o' that be'ind,
For a piece o' twisty rag
An' a goatskin water-bag
Was all the field-equipment 'e could find.
When the sweatin' troop-train lay
In a sidin' through the day,
Where the 'eat would make your bloomin' eyebrows crawl,
We shouted 'Harry By!'[2]
Till our throats were bricky-dry,
Then we wopped 'im 'cause 'e couldn't serve us all.
    It was 'Din! Din! Din!
    You 'eathen, where the mischief 'ave you been?
    You put some juldee[3] in it
    Or I'll marrow you this minute[4]
    If you don't fill up my helmet, Gunga Din!

---

[1] Bring water swiftly.
[2] Mr. Atkins' equivalent for 'O brother.'
[3] Be quick.   [4] Hit you.

'E would dot an' carry one
    Till the longest day was done;
An' 'e didn't seem to know the use o' fear.
    If we charged or broke or cut,
    You could bet your bloomin' nut,
'E'd be waitin' fifty paces right flank rear.
    With 'is mussick[1] on 'is back,
    'E would skip with our attack,
An' watch us till the bugles made 'Retire,'
    An' for all 'is dirty 'ide
    'E was white, clear white, inside
When 'e went to tend the wounded under fire!
        It was 'Din! Din! Din!'
  With the bullets kickin' dust-spots on the green.
        When the cartridges ran out,
        You could hear the front-files shout,
  'Hi! ammunition-mules an' Gunga Din!'

    I sha'n't forgit the night
    When I dropped be'ind the fight
With a bullet where my belt-plate should 'a' been.
    I was chokin' mad with thirst,
    An' the man that spied me first
Was our good old grinnin', gruntin' Gunga Din.
    'E lifted up my 'ead,
    An' he plugged me where I bled,
An' 'e guv me 'arf-a-pint o' water-green:
    It was crawlin' and it stunk,
    But of all the drinks I've drunk,
I'm gratefullest to one from Gunga Din.
        It was 'Din! Din! Din!'
  'Ere's a beggar with a bullet through 'is spleen;
        'E's chawin' up the ground,
        An' 'e's kickin' all around:
  For Gawd's sake git the water, Gunga Din!

    'E carried me away
    To where a dooli lay,
An' a bullet come an' drilled the beggar clean.
    'E put me safe inside,

---

[1] Water skin.

>   An' just before 'e died:
> 'I 'ope you liked your drink,' sez Gunga Din.
>   So I'll meet 'im later on
>   At the place where 'e is gone—
> Where it's always double drill and no canteen;
>   'E'll be squattin' on the coals,
>   Givin' drink to poor damned souls,
> An' I'll get a swig in hell from Gunga Din!
>   Yes, Din! Din! Din!
>   You Lazarushian-leather Gunga Din!
>   Though I've belted you and flayed you,
>   By the living Gawd that made you,
>   You're a better man than I am, Gunga Din!

Oonts

(NORTHERN INDIA TRANSPORT TRAIN)

Wot makes the soldier's 'eart to penk, wot makes him to perspire?
It isn't standin' up to charge nor lyin' down to fire;
But it's everlastin' waitin' on a everlastin' road
For the commissariat camel an' 'is commissariat load.
    O the oont,[1] O the oont, O the commissariat oont!
        With 'is silly neck a-bobbin' like a basket full o' snakes;
        We packs 'im like an idol, an' you ought to 'ear 'im grunt,
        An' when we gets 'im loaded up 'is blessed girth-rope breaks.

Wot makes the rear-guard swear so 'ard when night is drorin' in,
An' every native follower is shiverin' for 'is skin?
It ain't the chanst o' being rushed by Paythans from the 'ills,
It's the commissariat camel puttin' on 'is bloomin' frills!
    O the oont, O the oont, O the hairy scary oont!
        A-trippin' over tent-ropes when we've got the night alarm!
        We socks 'im with a stretcher-pole an' 'eads 'im off in front,
        An' when we've saved 'is bloomin' life 'e chaws our bloomin' arm.

The 'orse 'e knows above a bit, the bullock's but a fool,

---

[1] Camel—*oo* is pronounced like *u* in 'bull,' but by Mr. Atkins to rhyme with 'front.'

The elephant's a gentleman, the battery-mule's a mule;
But the commissariat cam-u-el, when all is said an' done,
'E's a devil an' a ostrich an' a orphan-child in one.
    O the oont, O the oont, O the Gawd-forsaken oont!
        The lumpy-'umpy 'ummin'-bird a-singin' where 'e lies,
      'E's blocked the whole division from the rear-guard to the front,
        An' when we get him up again—the beggar goes an' dies!

'E'll gall an' chafe an' lame an' fight—'e smells most awful vile;
'E'll lose 'isself for ever if you let 'im stray a mile;
'E's game to graze the 'ole day long an' 'owl the 'ole night through,
An' when 'e comes to greasy ground 'e splits 'isself in two.
    O the oont, O the oont, O the floppin', droppin' oont!
        When 'is long legs give from under an' 'is meltin' eye is dim,
      The tribes is up be'ind us, and the tribes is out in front—
        It ain't no jam for Tommy, but it's kites an' crows for 'im.

So when the cruel march is done, an' when the roads is blind,
An' when we sees the camp in front an' 'ears the shots be'ind,
Ho then we strips 'is saddle off, and all 'is woes is past:
'E thinks on us that used 'im so, and gets revenge at last.
    O the oont, O the oont, O the floatin', bloatin' oont!
        The late lamented camel in the water-cut 'e lies;
      We keeps a mile behind 'im an' we keeps a mile in front,
        But 'e gets into the drinkin'-casks, and then o' course we dies.

The Widow at Windsor

'Ave you 'eard o' the Widow at Windsor
    With a hairy gold crown on 'er 'ead?
She 'as ships on the foam—she 'as millions at 'ome,
    An' she pays us poor beggars in red.
       (Ow, poor beggars in red!)
There's 'er nick on the cavalry 'orses,
    There's 'er mark on the medical stores—
An' 'er troopers you'll find with a fair wind be'ind

That takes us to various wars.
    (Poor beggars!—barbarious wars!)

    Then 'ere's to the Widow at Windsor,
        An' 'ere's to the stores an' the guns,
    The men an' the 'orses what makes up the forces
        O' Missis Victorier's sons.
        (Poor beggars! Victorier's sons!)

Walk wide o' the Widow at Windsor,
    For 'alf o' Creation she owns:
We 'ave bought 'er the same with the sword an' the flame,
    An' we've salted it down with our bones.
        (Poor beggars!—it's blue with our bones!)
Hands off o' the sons of the Widow,
    Hands off o' the goods in 'er shop,
For the Kings must come down an' the Emperors frown
    When the Widow at Windsor says 'Stop'!
        (Poor Beggars!—we're sent to say 'Stop'!)

    Then 'ere's to the Lodge o' the Widow,
        From the Pole to the Tropics it runs—
    To the Lodge that we tile with the rank an' the file,
        An' open in form with the guns.
        (Poor beggars!—it's always they guns!)

We 'ave 'eard o' the Widow at Windsor,
    It's safest to leave 'er alone:
For 'er sentries we stand by the sea an' the land
    Wherever the bugles are blown.
        (Poor beggars!—an' don't we get blown!)
Take 'old o' the Wings o' the Mornin',
    An' flop round the earth till you're dead;
But you won't get away from the tune that they play
    To the bloomin' old Rag over'ead.
        (Poor beggars!—it's 'ot over'ead!)

    Then 'ere's to the sons o' the Widow
        Wherever, 'owever they roam.
    'Ere's all they desire, an' if they require
        A speedy return to their 'ome.
        (Poor beggars!—they'll never see 'ome!)

Mandalay

By the old Moulmein Pagoda, lookin' eastward to the sea,
There's a Burma girl a-settin', and I know she thinks o' me;
For the wind is in the palm-trees, and the temple-bells they say:
'Come you back, you British soldier; come you back to Mandalay!'

> Come you back to Mandalay,
> Where the old Flotilla lay:
> Can't you 'ear their paddles chunkin' from Rangoon to Mandalay?
> On the road to Mandalay,
> Where the flyin'-fishes play,
> An' the dawn comes up like thunder outer China 'crost the Bay!

'Er petticoat was yaller an' 'er little cap was green,
An' 'er name was Supi-yaw-lat—jes' the same as Theebaw's Queen,
An' I seed her first a-smokin' of a whackin' white cheroot,
An' a-wastin' Christian kisses on an 'eathen idol's foot:

> Bloomin' idol made o' mud—
> What they called the Great Gawd Budd—
> Plucky lot she cared for idols when I kissed 'er where she stud!
> On the road to Mandalay, etc.

When the mist was on the rice-fields an' the sun was droppin' slow,
She'd git 'er little banjo an' she'd sing *'Kulla-lo-lo!'*
With 'er arm upon my shoulder an' 'er cheek agin my cheek
We useter watch the steamers an' the *hathis* pilin' teak.

> Elephints a-pilin' teak
> In the sludgy, squdgy creek,
> Where the silence 'ung that 'eavy you was 'arf afraid to speak!
> On the road to Mandalay, etc.

But that's all shove be'ind me—long ago an' fur away,
An' there ain't no 'busses runnin' from the Bank to Mandalay;
An' I'm learnin' 'ere in London what the ten-year soldier tells:
'If you've 'eard the East a-callin', you won't never 'eed naught else.'

> No! you won't 'eed nothin' else
> But them spicy garlic smells,

>   An' the sunshine an' the palm-trees an' the tinkly temple-
>   bells;
>   On the road to Mandalay, etc.

I am sick o' wastin' leather on these gritty pavin'-stones,
An' the blasted Henglish drizzle wakes the fever in my bones;
Tho' I walks with fifty 'ousemaids outer Chelsea to the Strand,
An' they talks a lot o' lovin', but wot do they understand?

>   Beefy face an' grubby 'and—
>   Law! wot do they understand?
>   I've a neater, sweeter maiden in a cleaner, greener land!
>   On the road to Mandalay, etc.

Ship me somewheres east of Suez, where the best is like the worst,
Where there aren't no Ten Commandments an' a man can raise a
  thirst;
For the temple-bells are callin', and it's there that I would be—
By the old Moulmein Pagoda, looking lazy at the sea;

>   On the road to Mandalay,
>   Where the old Flotilla lay,
>   With our sick beneath the awnings when we went to Man-
>   dalay!
>   Oh the road to Mandalay,
>   Where the flyin'-fishes play,
>   An' the dawn comes up like thunder outer China 'crost
>   the Bay!

Gentlemen-Rankers

To the legion of the lost ones, to the cohort of the damned,
  To my brethren in their sorrow overseas,
Sings a gentleman of England cleanly bred, machinely crammed,
  And a trooper of the Empress, if you please.
Yea, a trooper of the forces who has run his own six horses,
  And faith he went the pace and went it blind,
And the world was more than kin while he held the ready tin,
  But to-day the Sergeant's something less than kind.
>   We're poor little lambs who've lost our way,
>   Baa! Baa! Baa!
>   We're little black sheep who've gone astray,

> Baa—aa—aa!
> Gentlemen-rankers out on the spree
> Damned from here to Eternity,
> God ha' mercy on such as we,
> > Baa! Yah! Bah!

Oh, it's sweet to sweat through stables, sweet to empty kitchen slops,
    And it's sweet to hear the tales the troopers tell,
To dance with blowzy housemaids at the regimental hops,
    And thrash the cad who says you waltz too well.
Yes, it makes you cock-a-hoop to be 'Rider' to your troop,
    And branded with a blasted worsted spur,
When you envy, Oh, how keenly, one poor Tommy being cleanly
    Who blacks your boots and sometimes call you 'Sir.'

If the home we never write to, and the oaths we never keep,
    And all we know most distant and most dear,
Across the snoring barrack-room return to break our sleep,
    Can you blame us if we soak ourselves in beer?
When the drunken comrade mutters and the great guard-lantern gutters
    And the horror of our fall is written plain,
Every secret, self-revealing on the aching white-washed ceiling,
    Do you wonder that we drug ourselves from pain?

We have done with Hope and Honour, we are lost to Love and Truth,
    We are dropping down the ladder rung by rung,
And the measure of our torment is the measure of our youth.
    God help us, for we knew the worst too young!
Our shame is clean repentance for the crime that brought the sentence,
    Our pride it is to know no spur of pride,
And the Curse of Reuben holds us till an alien turf enfolds us
    And we die, and none can tell Them where we died.

> We're poor little lambs who've lost our way,
> > Baa! Baa! Baa!
>
> We're little black sheep who've gone astray,
> > Baa—aa—aa!
>
> Gentlemen-rankers out on the spree,
> Damned from here to Eternity,
> God ha' mercy on such as we,
> > Baa! Yah! Bah!

L'Envoi
(TO 'BARRACK-ROOM BALLADS')

There's a whisper down the field where the year has shot her yield,
  And the ricks stand grey to the sun,
Singing:—'Over then, come over, for the bee has quit the clover,
  And your English summer's done.'

> You have heard the beat of the off-shore wind,
> And the thresh of the deep-sea rain;
> You have heard the song—how long! how long?
> Pull out on the trail again!

> Ha' done with the Tents of Shem, dear lass,
> We've seen the seasons through,
> And it's time to turn on the old trail, our own trail, the out trail,
> Pull out, pull out, on the Long Trail—the trail that is always new.

It's North you may run to the rime-ringed sun
  Or South to the blind Horn's hate;
Or East all the way into Mississippi Bay,
  Or West to the Golden Gate;

> Where the blindest bluffs hold good, dear lass,
> And the wildest tales are true,
> And the men bulk big on the old trail, our own trail, the out trail,
> And life runs large on the Long Trail—the trail that is always new.

The days are sick and cold, and the skies are grey and old,
  And the twice-breathed airs blow damp;
And I'd sell my tired soul for the bucking beam-sea roll
  Of a black Bilbao tramp;

> With her load-line over her hatch, dear lass,
> And a drunken Dago crew,
> And her nose held down on the old trail, our own trail, the out trail
> From Cadiz Bar on the Long Trail—the trail that is always new.

There be triple ways to take, of the eagle or the snake,
    Or the way of a man with a maid;
But the sweetest way to me is a ship's upon the sea
    In the heel of the North-East Trade.

> Can you hear the crash on her bows, dear lass,
> And the drum of the racing screw,
> As she ships it green on the old trail, our own trail, the out trail,
> As she lifts and 'scends on the Long Trail—the trail that is always new?

See the shaking funnels roar, with the Peter at the fore,
    And the fenders grind and heave,
And the derricks clack and grate as the tackle hooks the crate,
    And the fall-rope whines through the sheave;

> It's 'Gang-plank up and in,' dear lass,
> It's 'Hawsers warp her through!'
> And it's 'All clear aft' on the old trail, our own trail, the out trail,
> We're backing down on the Long Trail—the trail that is always new.

Oh, the mutter overside, when the port-fog holds us tied,
    And the syrens hoot their dread!
When foot by foot we creep o'er the hueless viewless deep
    To the sob of the questing lead!

> It's down by the Lower Hope, dear lass,
> With the Gunfleet Sands in view,
> Till the Mouse swings green on the old trail, our own trail, the out trail,
> And the Gull Light lifts on the Long Trail—the trail that is always new.

Oh, the blazing tropic night, when the wake's a welt of light
    That holds the hot sky tame,
And the steady fore-foot snores through the planet-powdered floors
    Where the scared whale flukes in flame!

> Her plates are scarred by the sun, dear lass,
> Her ropes are taunt with the dew,
> For we're booming down on the old trail, our own trail, the out trail,

> We're sagging south on the Long Trail — the trail that is
> always new.

Then home, get her home where the drunken rollers comb,
   And the shouting seas drive by,
And the engines stamp and ring and the wet bows reel and swing,
   And the Southern Cross rides high!

> Yes, the old lost stars wheel back, dear lass,
> That blaze in the velvet blue.
> They're all old friends on the old trail, our own trail, the out
> trail,
> They're God's own guides on the Long Trail—the trail that is
> always new.

Fly forward, O my heart, from the Foreland to the Start—
   We're steaming all too slow,
And it's twenty thousand miles to our little lazy isle
   Where the trumpet-orchids blow!

> You have heard the call of the off-shore wind
> And the voice of the deep-sea rain—
> You have heard the song—how long! how long?
> Pull out on the trail again!

> The Lord knows what we may find, dear lass,
> And the Deuce knows what we may do—
> But we're back once more on the old trail, our own trail, the
> out trail,
> We're down, hull-down on the Long Trail—the trail that is
> always new.

McAndrew's Hymn

Lord, Thou hast made this world below the shadow of a dream,
An', taught by time, I tak' it so—exceptin' always Steam.
From coupler-flange to spindle-guide I see Thy Hand, O God—
Predestination in the stride o' yon connectin'-rod.
John Calvin might ha' forged the same—enorrmous, certain,
   slow—
Ay, wrought it in the furnace-flame—*my* "Institutio."
I cannot get my sleep to-night; old bones are hard to please;
I'll stand the middle watch up here—alone wi' God an' these

My engines, after ninety days o' race an' rack an' strain
Through all the seas of all Thy world, slam-bangin' home again.
Slam-bang too much—they knock a wee—the crosshead-gibs are loose;
But thirty thousand mile o' sea has gied them fair excuse. . . .
Fine, clear an' dark—a full-draught breeze, wi' Ushant out o' sight,
An' Ferguson relievin' Hay. Old girl, ye'll walk to-night!
His wife's at Plymouth. . . . Seventy—One—Two—Three since he began—
Three turns for Mistress Ferguson. . . . an' who's to blame the man?
There's none at any port for me, by drivin' fast or slow,
Since Elsie Campbell went to Thee, Lord, thirty years ago.
(The year the *Sarah Sands* was burned. Oh roads we used to tread,
Fra' Maryhill to Pollokshaws—fra' Govan to Parkhead!)
Not but they're ceevil on the Board. Ye'll hear Sir Kenneth say:
"Good morrn, McAndrews! Back again? An' how's your bilge to-day?"
Miscallin' technicalities but handin' me my chair
To drink Madeira wi' three Earls—the auld Fleet Engineer,
That started as a boiler-whelp—when steam and he were low.
I mind the time we used to serve a broken pipe wi' tow.
Ten pound was all the pressure then—Eh! Eh!—a man wad drive;
An' here, our workin' gauges give one hunder' fifty-five!
We're creepin' on wi' each new rig—less weight an' larger power:
There'll be the loco-boiler next an' thirty knots an hour!
Thirty an' more. What I ha' seen since ocean-steam began
Leaves me no doot for the machine: but what about the man?
The man that counts, wi' all his runs, one million mile o' sea:
Four time the span from earth to moon. . . . How far, O Lord, from Thee?
That wast beside him night an' day. Ye mind my first typhoon?
It scoughed the skipper on his way to jock wi' the saloon.
Three feet were on the stokehold floor—just slappin' to an' fro—
An' cast me on a furnace-door. I have the marks to show.
Marks! I ha' marks o' more than burns—deep in my soul an' black,
An' times like this, when things go smooth, my wickudness comes back.
The sins o' four and forty years, all up an' down the seas,
Clack an' repeat like valves half-fed. . . . Forgie's our trespasses.
Nights when I'd come on deck to mark, wi' envy in my gaze,
The couples kittlin' in the dark between the funnel stays;
Years when I raked the ports wi' pride to fill my cup o' wrong—

Judge not, O Lord, my steps aside at Gay Street in Hong-Kong!
Blot out the wastrel hours of mine in sin when I abode—
Jane Harrigan's an' Number Nine, The Reddick an' Grant Road!
An' waur than all—my crownin' sin—rank blasphemy an' wild.
I was not four and twenty then—Ye wadna judge a child?
I'd seen the Tropics first that run—new fruit, new smells, new air—
How could I tell—blind-fou wi' sun—the Deil was lurkin' there?
By day like playhouse-scenes the shore slid past our sleepy eyes;
By night those soft, lasceevious stars leered from those velvet skies,
In port (we used no cargo-steam) I'd daunder down the streets—
An ijjit grinnin' in a dream—for shells an' parrakeets,
An' walkin'-sticks o' carved bamboo an' blowfish stuffed an' dried—
Fillin' my bunk wi' rubbishry the Chief put overside.
Till, off Sumbawa Head, Ye mind, I heard a landbreeze ca',
Milk-warm wi' breath o' spice an' bloom: "McAndrews, come awa'!"
Firm, clear an' low—no haste, no hate—the ghostly whisper went,
Just statin' eevidential facts beyon' all argument:
"Your mither's God's a graspin' deil, the shadow o' yoursel',
"Got out o' books by meenisters clean daft on Heaven an' Hell.
"They mak' him in the Broomielaw, o' Glasgie cold an' dirt,
"A jealous, pridefu' fetich, lad, that's only strong to hurt,
"Ye'll not go back to Him again an' kiss His red-hot rod,
"But come wi' Us" (Now, who were *They?*) "an' know the Leevin' God,
"That does not kipper souls for sport or break a life in jest,
"But swells the ripenin' cocoanuts an' ripes the woman's breast."
An' there it stopped: cut off: no more; that quiet, certain voice—
For me, six months o' twenty-four, to leave or take at choice.
'Twas on me like a thunderclap—it racked me through an' through—
Temptation past the show o' speech, unnamable an' new—
The Sin against the Holy Ghost? . . . An' under all, our screw.
That storm blew by but left behind her anchor-shiftin' swell,
Thou knowest all my heart an' mind, Thou knowest, Lord, I fell.
Third on the *Mary Gloster* then, and first that night in Hell!
Yet was Thy hand beneath my head: about my feet Thy care—
Fra' Deli clear to Torres Strait, the trial o' despair,
But when we touched the Barrier Reef Thy answer to my prayer!
We dared na run that sea by night but lay an' held our fire,
An' I was drowzin' on the hatch—sick—sick wi' doubt an' tire:
"Better the sight of eyes that see than wanderin' o' desire!"
Ye mind that word? Clear as our gongs—again, an' once again,

When rippin' down through coral-trash ran out our moorin'-chain;
An' by Thy Grace I had the Light to see my duty plain.
Light on the engine-room—no more—clear as our carbons burn.
I've lost it since a thousand times, but never past return.

. . . .

Obsairve! Per annum we'll have here two thousand souls aboard—
Think not I dare to justify myself before the Lord,
But—average fifteen hunder' souls safe-borne fra port to port—
I *am* o' service to my kind. Ye wadna' blame the thought?
Maybe they steam from grace to wrath—to sin by folly led,—
It isna mine to judge their path—their lives are on my head.
Mine at the last—when all is done it all comes back to me,
The fault that leaves six thousand ton a log upon the sea.
We'll tak' one stretch—three weeks an' odd by any road ye steer—
Fra' Cape Town east to Wellington—ye need an engineer.
Fail there—ye've time to weld your shaft—ay, eat it, ere ye're spoke,
Or make Kerguelen under sail—three jiggers burned wi' smoke!
An' home again, the Rio run: it's no child's play to go
Steamin' to bell for fourteen days o' snow an' floe an' blow—
The bergs like kelpies overside that girn an' turn an' shift
Whaur, grindin' like the Mills o' God, goes by the big South drift.
(Hail, snow an' ice that praise the Lord: I've met them at their work,
An' wished we had anither route or they anither kirk.)
Yon's strain, hard strain, o' head an' hand, for though Thy Power brings
All skill to naught, Ye'll understand a man must think o' things.
Then, at the last, we'll get to port an' hoist their baggage clear—
The passengers, wi' gloves an' canes—an' this is what I'll hear:
"Well, thank ye for a pleasant voyage. The tender's comin' now."
While I go testin' follower-bolts an' watch the skipper bow.
They've words for everyone but me—shake hands wi' half the crew,
Except the dour Scots engineer, the man they never knew.
An' yet I like the wark for all we've dam' few pickin's here—
No pension, an' the most we earn's four hunder' pound a year.
Better myself abroad? Maybe. *I'd* sooner starve than sail
Wi' such as call a snifter-rod *ross*. . . . French for nightingale.
Commeesion on my stores? Some do; but I can not afford
To lie like stewards wi' patty-pans. I'm older than the Board.
A bonus on the coal I save? Ou ay, the Scots are close,

But when I grudge the strength Ye gave I'll grudge their food to *those*.
(There's bricks that I might recommend—an' clink the fire-bars
   cruel.
No! Welsh—Wangarti at the worst—an' damn all patent fuel!)
Inventions? Ye must stay in port to mak' a patent pay.
My Deeferential Valve-Gear taught me how that business lay,
I blame no chaps wi' clearer head for aught they make or sell.
I found that I could not invent an' look to these—as well.
So, wrestled wi' Apollyon—Nah!—fretted like a bairn—
But burned the workin'-plans last run wi' all I hoped to earn.
Ye know how hard an Idol dies, an' what that meant to me—
E'en tak' it for a sacrifice acceptable to Thee. . . .
Below there! Oiler! What's your wark? Ye find her runnin' hard?
Ye needn't swill the cap wi' oil—this isn't the Cunard.
Ye thought? Ye are not paid to think. Go, sweat that off again!
Tck! Tck! It's deeficult to sweer nor tak' The Name in vain!
Men, ay an' women, call me stern. Wi' these to oversee
Ye'll note I've little time to burn on social repartee.
The bairns see what their elders miss; they'll hunt me to an' fro,
Till for the sake of—well, a kiss—I tak' 'em down below.
That minds me of our Viscount loon—Sir Kenneth's kin—the chap
Wi' russia leather tennis-shoon an' spar-decked yachtin'-cap.
I showed him round last week, o'er all—an' at the last says he:
"Mister McAndrews, don't you think steam spoils romance at sea?"
Damned ijjit! I'd been doon that morn to see what ailed the throws,
Manholin', on my back—the cranks three inches from my nose.
Romance! Those first-class passengers they like it very well,
Printed an' bound in little books; but why don't poets tell?
I'm sick of all their quirks an' turns—the loves an' doves they
   dream—
Lord, send a man like Robbie Burns to sing the Song o' Steam!
To match wi' Scotia's noblest speech yon orchestra sublime
Whaurto—uplifted like the Just—the tail-rods mark the time.
The crank-throws give the double-bass; the feed-pump sobs an'
   heaves:
An' now the main eccentrics start their quarrel on the sheaves.
Her time, her own appointed time, the rocking link-head bides,
Till—hear that note?—the rod's return whings glimmerin' through
   the guides.
They're all awa! True beat, full power, the clangin' chorus goes
Clear to the tunnel where they sit, my purrin' dynamoes.

Interdependence absolute, foreseen, ordained, decreed,
To work, Ye'll note, at any tilt an' every rate o' speed.
Fra skylight-lift to furnace-bars, backed, bolted, braced an' stayed,
An' singin' like the Mornin' Stars for joy that they are made;
While, out o' touch o' vanity, the sweatin' thrust-block says:
"Not unto us the praise, or man—not unto us the praise!"
Now, a' together, hear them lift their lesson—theirs an' mine:
"Law, Orrder, Duty an' Restraint, Obedience, Discipline!"
Mill, forge an' try-pit taught them that when roarin' they arose,
An' whiles I wonder if a soul was gied them wi' the blows.
Oh for a man to weld it then, in one trip-hammer strain,
Till even first-class passengers could tell the meanin' plain!
But no one cares except mysel' that serve an' understand
My seven thousand horse-power here. Eh, Lord! They're grand—
    they're grand!
Uplift am I? When first in store the new-made beasties stood,
Were Ye cast down that breathed the Word declarin' all things good?
Not so! O' that warld-liftin' joy no after-fall could vex,
Ye've left a glimmer still to cheer the Man—the Arrtifex!
That holds, in spite o' knock and scale, o' friction, waste an' slip,
An' by that light—now, mark my word—we'll build the Perfect
    Ship.
I'll never last to judge her lines or take her curve—not I.
But I ha' lived an' I ha' worked. All thanks to Thee, Most High!
An' I ha' done what I ha' done—judge Thou if ill or well—
Always Thy Grace preventin' me. . . .
                                  Losh! Yon's the "Stand by" bell.
Pilot so soon? His flare it is. The mornin'-watch is set.
Well, God be thanked, as I was sayin', I'm no Pelagian yet.
Now I'll tak' on. . . .
   'Morrn, Ferguson. Man, have ye ever thought
What your good leddy costs in coal? . . . I'll burn em down to port.

Sestina of the Tramp-Royal

Speakin' in general, I 'ave tried 'em all,
The 'appy roads that take you o'er the world.
Speakin' in general, I 'ave found them good

For such as cannot use one bed too long,
But must get 'ence, the same as I 'ave done,
An' go observin' matters till they die.

What do it matter where or 'ow we die,
So long as we've our 'ealth to watch it all—
The different ways that different things are done,
An' men an' women lovin' in this world—
Takin' our chances as they come along,
An' when they ain't, pretendin' they are good?

In cash or credit—no, it ain't no good;
You 'ave to 'ave the 'abit or you'd die,
Unless you lived your life but one day long,
Nor didn't prophesy nor fret at all,
But drew your tucker some'ow from the world,
An' never bothered what you might ha' done.

But, Gawd, what things are they I 'aven't done?
I've turned my 'and to most, an' turned it good,
In various situations round the world—
For 'im that doth not work must surely die;
But that's no reason man should labour all
'Is life on one same shift; life's none so long.

Therfore, from job to job I've moved along.
Pay couldn't 'old me when my time was done,
For something in my 'ead upset me all,
Till I 'ad dropped whatever 'twas for good,
An', out at sea, be'eld the dock-lights die,
An' met my mate—the wind that tramps the world.

It's like a book, I think, this bloomin' world,
Which you can read and care for just so long,
But presently you feel that you will die
Unless you get the page you're readin' done,
An' turn another—likely not so good;
But what you're after is to turn 'em all.

Gawd bless this world! Whatever she 'ath done—
Excep' when awful long—I've found it good.
So write, before I die, " 'E liked it all!"

When 'Omer smote 'is bloomin' lyre,
  He'd 'eard men sing by land an' sea;
An' what he thought 'e might require,
  'E went an' took—the same as me!

The market-girls an' fishermen,
  The shepherds an' the sailors, too,
They 'eard old songs turn up again,
  But kep' it quiet—same as you!

They knew 'e stole; 'e knew they knowed.
  They didn't tell, nor make a fuss,
But winked at 'Omer down the road,
  An' 'e winked back—the same as us!

The Ladies

I've taken my fun where I've found it;
  I've rogued an' I've ranged in my time;
I've 'ad my pickin' o' sweet'earts,
  An' four o' the lot was prime.
One was an 'arf-caste widow,
  One was a woman at Prome,
One was the wife of a *jemadar-sais*,*
  An' one is a girl at 'ome.

Now I aren't no 'and with the ladies,
  For, takin' 'em all along,
You never can say till you ve tried 'em,
  An' then you are like to be wrong.
There's times when you'll think that you mightn't,
  There's times when you'll know that you might;
But the things you will learn from the Yellow an' Brown,
  They'll 'elp you an 'eap with the White!

I was a young un at 'Oogli,
  Shy as a girl to begin;
Aggie de Castrer she made me,

---

* Head-groom.

    An' Aggie was clever as sin;
Older than me, but my first un—
    More like a mother she were—
Showed me the way to promotion an' pay,
    An' I learned about women from 'er.

Then I was ordered to Burma,
    Actin' in charge o' Bazar,
An' I got me a tiddy live 'eathen
    Through buyin' supplies off 'er pa.
Funny an' yellow an' faithful—
    Doll in a teacup she were,
But we lived on the square, like a true-married pair,
    An' I learned about women from 'er.

Then we was shifted to Neemuch
    (Or I might ha' been keepin' 'er now),
An' I took with a shiny she-devil,
    The wife of a nigger at Mhow;
'Taught me the gipsy-folks' *bolee*;*
    Kind o' volcano she were,
For she knifed me one night 'cause I wished she was white,
    And I learned about women from 'er.

Then I come 'ome in the trooper,
    'Long of a kid o' sixteen—
Girl from a convent at Meerut,
    The straightest I ever 'ave seen.
Love at first sight was 'er trouble,
    She didn't know what it were;
An' I wouldn't do such, 'cause I liked 'er too much,
    But—I learned about women from 'er!

I've taken my fun where I've found it,
    An' now I must pay for my fun,
For the more you 'ave known o' the others
    The less will you settle to one;
An' the end of it's sittin' and thinkin',
    An' dreamin' Hell-fires to see;
So be warned by my lot (which I know you will not),
    An' learn about women from me!

* Slang.

What did the colonel's lady think?
  Nobody never knew.
Somebody asked the sergeant's wife,
  An' she told 'em true.
When you get to a man in the case,
  They're like as a row of pins—
For the colonel's lady an' Judy O'Grady
  Are sisters under their skins!

The Sergeant's Weddin'

'E was warned agin 'er—
  That's what made 'im look;
She was warned agin 'im—
  That is why she took.
'Wouldn't 'ear no reason,
  'Went an' done it blind;
We know all about 'em,
  They've got all to find!

>   Cheer for the Sergeant's weddin'—
>   Give 'em one cheer more!
>   Gray gun-'orses in the lando,
>   An' a rogue is married to, etc.

What's the use o' tellin'
  'Arf the lot she's been?
'E's a bloomin' robber,
  An' 'e keeps canteen.
'Ow did 'e get 'is buggy?
  Gawd, you needn't ask!
Made 'is forty gallon
  Out of every cask!

Watch 'im, with 'is 'air cut,
  Count us filin' by—
Won't the Colonel praise 'is
  Pop—u—lar—i—ty!
We 'ave scores to settle—
  Scores for more than beer;

She's the girl to pay 'em—
   That is why we're 'ere!

See the chaplain thinkin'?
   See the women smile?
Twig the married winkin'
   As they take the aisle?
Keep your side-arms quiet,
   Dressin' by the Band.
Ho! You 'oly beggars,
   Cough be'ind your 'and!

Now it's done an' over,
   'Ear the organ squeak,
"Voice that breathed o'er Eden"—
   Ain't she got the cheek!
White an' laylock ribbons,
   Think yourself so fine!
I'd pray Gawd to take yer
   'Fore I made yer mine!

Escort to the kerridge,
   Wish 'im luck, the brute!
Chuck the slippers after—
   [Pity 'taint a boot!]
Bowin' like a lady,
   Blushin' like a lad—
'Oo would say to see 'em—
   Both are rotten bad!

> *Cheer for the Sergeant's weddin'—*
>   *Give 'em one cheer more!*
> *Gray gun-'orses in the lando,*
>   *An' a rogue is married to, etc.*

The 'Eathen

The 'eathen in 'is blindness bows down to wood an' stone;
'E don't obey no orders unless they is 'is own;
'E keeps 'is side-arms awful: 'e leaves 'em all about,
An' then comes up the regiment an' pokes the 'eathen out.

*All along o' dirtiness, all along o' mess,
All along o' doin' things rather-more-or-less,
All along of abby-nay,* kul,† and hazar-ho,‡
Mind you keep your rifle an' yourself jus' so!*

The young recruit is 'aughty—'e draf's from Gawd knows where;
They bid 'im show 'is stockin's an' lay 'is mattress square;
'E calls it bloomin' nonsense—'e doesn't know, no more—
An' then up comes 'is company an' kicks 'em round the floor!

The young recruit is 'ammered—'e takes it very 'ard;
'E 'angs 'is 'ead an' mutters—'e sulks about the yard;
'E talks o' "cruel tyrants" 'e'll swing for by-an'-bye,
An' the others 'ears an' mocks 'im, an' the boy goes orf to cry.

The young recruit is silly—'e thinks o' suicide;
'E's lost 'is gutter-devil; 'e 'asn't got 'is pride;
But day by day they kicks 'im, which 'elps 'im on a bit,
'Till 'e finds 'isself one mornin' with a full an' proper kit.

*Gettin' clear o' dirtiness, gettin' done with mess,
Gettin' shut o' doin' things rather-more-or-less;
Not so fond of abby-nay, kul, nor hazar-ho,
Learns to keep 'is rifle an' 'isself jus' so!*

The young recruit is 'appy—'e throws a chest to suit;
You see 'im grow mustaches; you 'ear 'im slap 'is boot;
'E learns to drop the "bloodies" from every word he slings,
An' 'e shows an 'ealthy brisket when 'e strips for bars an' rings.

The cruel tyrant sergeants they watch 'im 'arf a year;
They watch 'im with 'is comrades, they watch 'im with 'is beer;
They watch 'im with the women, at the regimental dance,
And the cruel tyrant sergeants send 'is name along for "Lance."

An' now 'e's 'arf o' nothin', an' all a private yet,
'Is room they up an' rags 'im to see what they will get;
They rags 'im low an' cunnin', each dirty trick they can,
But 'e learns to sweat 'is temper an' 'e learns to know 'is man.

An', last, a Colour-Sergeant, as such to be obeyed,
'E leads 'is men at cricket, 'e leads 'em on parade;

---

* Not now.   † To-morrow.   ‡ Wait a bit.

They sees 'em quick an' 'andy, uncommon set an' smart,
An' so 'e talks to orficers which 'ave the Core at 'eart.

'E learns to do 'is watchin' without it showin' plain;
'E learns to save a dummy, an' shove 'im straight again;
'E learns to check a ranker that's buyin' leave to shirk;
An' 'e learns to make men like 'im so they'll learn to like their work.

An' when it comes to marchin' he'll see their socks are right,
An' when it comes to action 'e shows 'em 'ow to sight;
'E knows their ways of thinkin' and just what's in their mind;
'E feels when they are comin' on an' when they've fell be'ind.

'E knows each talkin' corpril that leads a squad astray;
'E feels 'is innards 'eavin', 'is bowels givin' way;
'E sees the blue-white faces all tryin' 'ard to grin,
An' 'e stands an' waits an' suffers till it's time to cap 'em in.

An' now the hugly bullets come peckin' through the dust,
An' no one wants to face 'em, but every beggar must;
So, like a man in irons which isn't glad to go,
They moves 'em off by companies uncommon stiff an' slow.

Of all 'is five years' schoolin' they don't remember much
Excep' the not retreatin', the step an' keepin' touch.
It looks like teachin' wasted when they duck an' spread an' 'op,
But if 'e 'adn't learned 'em they'd be all about the shop!

An' now it's " 'Oo goes backward?" an' now it's " 'Oo comes on?"
An' now it's "Get the doolies," an' now the captain's gone;
An' now it's bloody murder, but all the while they 'ear
'Is voice, the same as barrick drill, a-shepherdin' the rear.

'E's just as sick as they are, 'is 'eart is like to split,
But 'e works 'em, works 'em, works 'em till 'e feels 'em take the bit;
The rest is 'oldin' steady till the watchful bugles play,
An' 'e lifts 'em, lifts 'em, lifts 'em through the charge that wins the day!

> The 'eathen in 'is blindness bows down to wood an' stone;
> 'E don't obey no orders unless they is 'is own;
> The 'eathen in 'is blindness must end where 'e began,
> But the backbone of the Army is the noncommissioned man!

Keep away from dirtiness—keep away from mess.
Don't get into doin' things rather-more-or-less!
Let's ha' done with abby-nay, kul, an' hazar-ho;
Mind you keep your rifle an' yourself jus' so!

L'Envoi

(TO 'THE SEVEN SEAS')

When Earth's last picture is painted, and the tubes are twisted and dried,
When the oldest colours have faded, and the youngest critic has died,
We shall rest, and, faith, we shall need it—lie down for an æon or two,
Till the Master of All Good Workmen shall set us to work anew!

And those that were good shall be happy: they shall sit in a golden chair;
They shall splash at a ten-league canvas with brushes of comets' hair;
They shall find real saints to draw from—Magdalene, Peter, and Paul,
They shall work for an age at a sitting and never be tired at all!

And only the Master shall praise us, and only the Master shall blame;
And no one shall work for money, and no one shall work for fame;
But each for the joy of the working, and each, in his separate star,
Shall draw the Thing as he sees It for the God of Things as They Are!

The Sea and the Hills

Who hath desired the Sea?—the sight of salt water unbounded—
The heave and the halt and the hurl and the crash of the comber wind-hounded?
The sleek-barrelled swell before storm, grey, foamless, enormous, and growing—

Stark calm on the lap of the Line or the crazy-eyed hurricane
    blowing—
His Sea in no showing the same—his Sea and the same 'neath each
    showing:
        His Sea as she slackens or thrills?
So and no otherwise—so and no otherwise hillmen desire their
    Hills!

Who hath desired the Sea?—the immense and contemptuous
    surges?
The shudder, the stumble, the swerve, as the star-stabbing bowsprit
    emerges?
The orderly clouds of the Trades, the ridged, roaring sapphire
    thereunder—
Unheralded cliff-haunting flaws and the headsail's low-volleying
    thunder—
His Sea in no wonder the same—his Sea and the same through each
    wonder:
        His Sea as she rages or stills?
So and no otherwise—so and no otherwise hillmen desire their
    Hills.

Who hath desired the Sea? Her menaces swift as her mercies?
The in-rolling walls of the fog and the silver-winged breeze that
    disperses?
The unstable mined berg going South and the calvings and groans
    that declare it—
White water half-guessed overside and the moon breaking timely to
    bare it—
His Sea as his fathers have dared—his Sea as his children shall
    dare it:
        His Sea as she serves him or kills?
So and no otherwise—so and no otherwise hillmen desire their
    Hills.

Who hath desired the Sea? Her excellent loneliness rather
Than forecourts of kings, and her outermost pits than the streets
    where men gather
Inland, among dust, under trees—inland where the slayer may slay
    him—
Inland, out of reach of her arms, and the bosom whereon he must
    lay him—

His Sea from the first that betrayed—at the last that shall never
  betray him:
    His Sea that his being fulfils?
So and no otherwise—so and no otherwise hillmen desire their
  Hills.

The White Man's Burden

Take up the White Man's burden—
  Send forth the best ye breed—
Go bind your sons to exile
  To serve your captives' need;
To wait in heavy harness
  On fluttered folk and wild—
Your new-caught, sullen peoples,
  Half-devil and half-child.

Take up the White Man's burden—
  In patience to abide,
To veil the threat of terror
  And check the show of pride;
By open speech and simple,
  An hundred times made plain.
To seek another's profit,
  And work another's gain.

Take up the White Man's burden—
  The savage wars of peace—
Fill full the mouth of Famine
  And bid the sickness cease;
And when your goal is nearest
  The end for others sought,
Watch Sloth and heathen Folly
  Bring all your hope to nought.

Take up the White Man's burden—
  No tawdry rule of kings,
But toil of serf and sweeper—
  The tale of common things.
The ports ye shall not enter,
  The roads ye shall not tread,

Go make them with your living,
   And mark them with your dead.

Take up the White Man's burden—
   And reap his old reward:
The blame of those ye better,
   The hate of those ye guard—
The cry of hosts ye humour
   (Ah, slowly!) toward the light:—
"Why brought ye us from bondage,
   "Our loved Egyptian night?"

Take up the White Man's burden—
   Ye dare not stoop to less—
Nor call too loud on Freedom
   To cloak your weariness;
By all ye cry or whisper,
   By all ye leave or do,
The silent, sullen peoples
   Shall weigh your Gods and you.

Take up the White Man's burden—
   Have done with childish days—
The lightly proffered laurel,
   The easy, ungrudged praise.
Comes now, to search your manhood
   Through all the thankless years,
Cold-edged with dear-bought wisdom,
   The judgment of your peers!

Boots

We're foot—slog—slog—slog—sloggin' over Africa—
Foot—foot—foot—foot—sloggin' over Africa—
(Boots—boots—boots—boots—movin' up an' down again!)
    There's no discharge in the war!

Seven—six—eleven—five—nine-an'-twenty mile to-day—
Four—eleven—seventeen—thirty-two the day before—
(Boots—boots—boots—boots—movin' up an' down again!)
    There's no discharge in the war!

Don't—don't—don't—don't—look at what's in front of you.
(Boots—boots—boots—boots—movin' up an' down again);
Men—men—men—men—men go mad with watchin' em,
    An' there's no discharge in the war!

Try—try—try—try—to think o' something different—
Oh—my—God—keep—me from goin' lunatic!
(Boots—boots—boots—boots—movin' up an' down again!)
    There's no discharge in the war!

Count—count—count—count—the bullets in the bandoliers.
If—your—eyes—drop—they will get atop o' you!
(Boots—boots—boots—boots—movin' up an' down again)—
    There's no discharge in the war!

We—can—stick—out—'unger, thirst, an' weariness,
But—not—not—not—not the chronic sight of 'em—
Boots—boots—boots—boots—movin' up an' down again,
    An' there's no discharge in the war!

'Tain't—so—bad—by—day because o' company,
But night—brings—long—strings—o' forty thousand million
Boots—boots—boots—boots—movin' up an' down again.
    There's no discharge in the war!

I—'ave—marched—six—weeks in 'Ell an' certify
It—is—not—fire—devils, dark, or anything,
But boots—boots—boots—boots—movin' up an' down again,
    An' there's no discharge in the war!

Cities and Thrones and Powers

Cities and Thrones and Powers,
    Stand in Time's eye,
Almost as long as flowers,
    Which daily die;
But, as new buds put forth
    To glad new men,
Out of the spent and unconsidered Earth
    The Cities rise again.

This season's Daffodil,
    She never hears,

What change, what chance, what chill,
   Cut down last year's:
But with bold countenance,
   And knowledge small,
Esteems her seven days' continuance,
   To be perpetual.

So Time that is o'er-kind,
   To all that be,
Ordains us e'en as blind,
   As bold as she:
That in our very death,
   And burial sure,
Shadow to shadow, well-persuaded, saith,
   'See how our works endure!'

Tarrant Moss

I closed and drew for my love's sake
   That now is false to me,
And I slew the Reiver of Tarrant Moss
   And set Dumeny free.

They have gone down, they have gone down,
   They are standing all arow—
Twenty knights in the peat-water,
   That never struck a blow!

Their armour shall not dull nor rust,
   Their flesh shall not decay,
For Tarrant Moss holds them in trust,
   Until the Judgment Day.

Their soul went from them in their youth,
   Ah God, that mine had gone,
Whenas I leaned on my love's truth
   And not on my sword alone!

Whenas I leaned on lad's belief
   And not on my naked blade—
And I slew a thief, and an honest thief,
   For the sake of a worthless maid.

They have laid the Reiver low in his place,
    They have set me up on high,
But the twenty knights in the peat-water
    Are luckier than I.

And ever they give me gold and praise
    And ever I mourn my loss—
For I struck the blow for my false love's sake
    And not for the Men of the Moss!

A Song to Mithras

(HYMN OF THE 30TH LEGION: CIRCA A.D. 350)

Mithras, God of the Morning, our trumpets waken the Wall!
'Rome is above the Nations, but Thou art over all!'
Now as the names are answered, and the guards are marched away,
Mithras, also a soldier, give us strength for the day!

Mithras, God of the Noontide, the heather swims in the heat.
Our helmets scorch our foreheads, our sandals burn our feet.
Now in the ungirt hour—now ere we blink and drowse,
Mithras, also a soldier, keep us true to our vows!

Mithras, God of the Sunset, low on the Western main—
Thou descending immortal, immortal to rise again!
Now when the watch is ended, now when the wine is drawn!
Mithras, also a soldier, keep us pure till the dawn!

Mithras, God of the Midnight, here where the great bull dies,
Look on thy children in darkness. Oh take our sacrifice!
Many roads thou hast fashioned—all of them lead to the Light:
Mithras, also a soldier, teach us to die aright!

Hadramauti

Who knows the heart of the Christian? How does he reason?
What are his measures and balances? Which is his season
For laughter, forbearance or bloodshed, and what devils move him
When he arises to smite us? I do not love him.

He invites the derision of strangers—he enters all places.
Booted, bareheaded he enters. With shouts and embraces
He asks of us news of the household whom we reckon nameless.
Certainly Allah created him forty-fold shameless.

So it is not in the Desert. One came to me weeping—
The Avenger of Blood on his track—I took him in keeping,
Demanding not whom he had slain, I refreshed him, I fed him
As he were even a brother. But Eblis had bred him.

He was the son of an ape, ill at ease in his clothing,
He talked with his head, hands and feet. I endured him with loathing.
Whatever his spirit conceived his countenance showed it
As a frog shows in a mud-puddle. Yet I abode it!

I fingered my beard and was dumb, in silence confronting him.
His soul was too shallow for silence, e'en with Death hunting him.
I said: "'Tis his weariness speaks,' but, when he had rested,
He chirped in my face like some sparrow, and, presently, jested!

Wherefore slew I that stranger? He brought me dishonour.
I saddled my mare, Bijli, I set him upon her.
I gave him rice and goat's flesh. He bared me to laughter.
When he was gone from my tent, swift I followed after,
Taking my sword in my hand. The hot wine had filled him.
Under the stars he mocked me—therefore I killed him!

The Law of the Jungle

Now this is the Law of the Jungle—as old and as true as the sky;
And the Wolf that shall keep it may prosper, but the Wolf that shall break it must die.

As the creeper that girdles the tree-trunk the Law runneth forward and back—
For the strength of the Pack is the Wolf, and the strength of the Wolf is the Pack.

Wash daily from nose-tip to tail-tip; drink deeply, but never too deep;

And remember the night is for hunting, and forget not the day is for sleep.

The Jackal may follow the Tiger, but, Cub, when thy whiskers are grown,
Remember the Wolf is a hunter—go forth and get food of thine own.

Keep peace with the Lords of the Jungle—the Tiger, the Panther, the Bear;
And trouble not Hathi the Silent, and mock not the Boar in his lair.

When Pack meets with Pack in the Jungle, and neither will go from the trail,
Lie down till the leaders have spoken—it may be fair words shall prevail.

When ye fight with a Wolf of the Pack, ye must fight him alone and afar,
Lest others take part in the quarrel, and the Pack be diminished by war.

The Lair of the Wolf is his refuge, and where he has made him his home,
Not even the Head Wolf may enter, not even the Council may come.

The Lair of the Wolf is his refuge, but where he has digged it too plain,
The Council shall send him a message, and so he shall change it again.

If ye kill before midnight, be silent, and wake not the woods with your bay,
Lest ye frighten the deer from the crops, and the brothers go empty away.

Ye may kill for yourselves, and your mates, and your cubs as they need, and ye can;
But kill not for pleasure of killing, and seven times never kill Man!

If ye plunder his Kill from a weaker, devour not all in thy pride;
Pack-Right is the right of the meanest; so leave him the head and the hide.

The Kill of the Pack is the meat of the Pack. Ye must eat where it lies;
And no one may carry away of that meat to his lair, or he dies.

The Kill of the Wolf is the meat of the Wolf. He may do what he will,

But, till he has given permission, the Pack may not eat of that Kill.

Cub-Right is the right of the Yearling. From all of his Pack he may claim
Full-gorge when the killer has eaten; and none may refuse him the same.

Lair-Right is the right of the Mother. From all of her year she may claim
One haunch of each kill for her litter; and none may deny her the same.

Cave-Right is the right of the Father—to hunt by himself for his own:
He is freed of all calls to the Pack; he is judged by the Council alone.

Because of his age and his cunning, because of his gripe and his paw,
In all that the Law leaveth open, the word of the Head Wolf is Law.

Now these are the Laws of the Jungle, and many and mighty are they;
But the head and the hoof of the Law and the haunch and the hump is—Obey!

If—

If you can keep your head when all about you
    Are losing theirs and blaming it on you,
If you can trust yourself when all men doubt you,
    But make allowance for their doubting too;
If you can wait and not be tired by waiting,
    Or being lied about, don't deal in lies,
Or being hated don't give way to hating,
    And yet don't look too good, nor talk too wise:

If you can dream—and not make dreams your master;
    If you can think—and not make thoughts your aim,
If you can meet with Triumph and Disaster
    And treat those two impostors just the same;
If you can bear to hear the truth you've spoken
    Twisted by knaves to make a trap for fools,
Or watch the things you gave your life to, broken,
    And stoop and build 'em up with worn-out tools:

If you can make one heap of all your winnings
   And risk it on one turn of pitch-and-toss,
And lose, and start again at your beginnings
   And never breathe a word about your loss;
If you can force your heart and nerve and sinew
   To serve your turn long after they are gone,
And so hold on when there is nothing in you
   Except the Will which says to them: 'Hold on!'

If you can talk with crowds and keep your virtue,
   Or walk with Kings—nor lose the common touch,
If neither foes nor loving friends can hurt you,
   If all men count with you, but none too much;
If you can fill the unforgiving minute
   With sixty seconds' worth of distance run,
Yours is the Earth and everything that's in it,
   And—which is more—you'll be a Man, my son!

I keep six honest serving-men
   (They taught me all I knew);
Their names are What and Why and When
   And How and Where and Who.
I send them over land and sea,
   I send them east and west;
But after they have worked for me,
   I give them all a rest.

I let them rest from nine till five,
   For I am busy then,
As well as breakfast, lunch, and tea,
   For they are hungry men.
But different folk have different views;
   I know a person small—
She keeps ten million serving-men,
   Who get no rest at all!
She sends 'em abroad on her own affairs,
   From the second she opens her eyes—
One million Hows, two million Wheres,
   And seven million Whys!

The Song of the Little Hunter

Ere Mor the Peacock flutters, ere the Monkey People cry,
    Ere Chil the Kite swoops down a furlong sheer,
Through the Jungle very softly flits a shadow and a sigh—
    He is Fear, O Little Hunter, he is Fear!
Very softly down the glade runs a waiting, watching shade,
    And the whisper spreads and widens far and near.
And the sweat is on thy brow, for he passes even now—
    He is Fear, O Little Hunter, he is Fear!

Ere the moon has climbed the mountain, ere the rocks are ribbed with light,
    When the downward-dipping trails are dank and drear,
Comes a breathing hard behind thee—snuffle-snuffle through the night—
    It is Fear, O Little Hunter, it is Fear!
On thy knees and draw the bow; bid the shrilling arrow go;
    In the empty, mocking thicket plunge the spear!
But thy hands are loosed and weak, and the blood has left thy cheek—
    It is Fear, O Little Hunter, it is Fear!

When the heat-cloud sucks the tempest, when the slivered pine-trees fall,
    When the blinding, blaring rain-squalls lash and veer,
Through the war-gongs of the thunder rings a voice more loud than all—
    It is Fear, O Little Hunter, it is Fear!
Now the spates are banked and deep; now the footless boulders leap—
    Now the lightning shows each littlest leaf-rib clear—
But thy throat is shut and dried, and thy heart against thy side
    Hammers: Fear, O Little Hunter—this is Fear!

Blue Roses

Roses red and roses white
Plucked I for my love's delight.
She would none of all my posies—
Bade me gather her blue roses.

Half the world I wandered through,
Seeking where such flowers grew.
Half the world unto my quest
Answered me with laugh and jest.

Home I came at wintertide,
But my silly love had died,
Seeking with her latest breath
Roses from the arms of Death.

It may be beyond the grave
She shall find what she would have.
Mine was but an idle quest—
Roses white and red are best.

Mother o' Mine

If I were hanged on the highest hill,
    Mother o' mine, O mother o' mine!
I know whose love would follow me still,
    Mother o' mine, O mother o' mine!

If I were drowned in the deepest sea,
    Mother o' mine, O mother o' mine!
I know whose tears would come down to me,
    Mother o' mine, O mother o' mine!

If I were damned of body and soul,
I know whose prayers would make me whole,
    Mother o' mine, O mother o' mine!

The Vampire

A fool there was and he made his prayer
(Even as you and I!)
To a rag and a bone and a hank of hair
(We called her the woman who did not care)
But the fool he called her his lady fair—
(Even as you and I!)

Oh, the years we waste and the tears we waste,
And the work of our head and hand
Belong to the woman who did not know
(And now we know that she never could know)
And did not understand.

A fool there was and his goods he spent
(Even as you and I!)
Honour and faith and a sure intent
(And it wasn't the least what the lady meant),
But a fool must follow his natural bent
(Even as you and I!)

Oh, the toil we lost and the spoil we lost,
And the excellent things we planned,
Belong to the woman who didn't know why
(And now we know that she never knew why)
And did not understand.

The fool was stripped to his foolish hide
(Even as you and I!)
Which she might have seen when she threw him aside
(But it isn't on record the lady tried)
So some of him lived but the most of him died
(Even as you and I!)

And it isn't the shame and it isn't the blame
That stings like a white hot brand,
It's coming to know that she never knew why
(Seeing at last she could never know why)
And never could understand.

Recessional

God of our fathers, known of old,
   Lord of our far-flung battle-line,
Beneath whose awful Hand we hold
   Dominion over palm and pine—
Lord God of Hosts, be with us yet,
Lest we forget—lest we forget!

The tumult and the shouting dies;
   The Captains and the Kings depart:
Still stands Thine ancient sacrifice,
   An humble and a contrite heart.
Lord God of Hosts, be with us yet,
Lest we forget—lest we forget!

Far-called, our navies melt away;
   On dune and headland sinks the fire:
Lo, all our pomp of yesterday
   Is one with Nineveh and Tyre!
Judge of the Nations, spare us yet,
Lest we forget—lest we forget!

If, drunk with sight of power, we loose
   Wild tongues that have not Thee in awe,
Such boastings as the Gentiles use,
   Or lesser breeds without the Law—
Lord God of Hosts, be with us yet,
Lest we forget—lest we forget!

For heathen heart that puts her trust
   In reeking tube and iron shard,
All valiant dust that builds on dust,
   And guarding, calls not Thee to guard,
For frantic boast and foolish word—
Thy mercy on Thy People, Lord!

                                            Amen.

The Absent-Minded Beggar

When you've shouted "Rule Britannia," when you've sung "God save
   the Queen"—
   When you've finished killing Kruger with your mouth—
Will you kindly drop a shilling in my little tambourine
   For a gentleman in kharki ordered South?
He's an absent-minded beggar, and his weaknesses are great—
   But we and Paul must take him as we find him—
He is out on active service, wiping something off a slate—
   And he's left a lot of little things behind him!
Duke's son—cook's son—son of a hundred kings—

(*Fifty thousand horse and foot going to Table Bay!*)
*Each of 'em doing his country's work (and who's to look after their
   things?)*
Pass the hat for your credit's sake, and pay—pay—pay!

There are girls he married secret, asking no permission to,
   For he knew he wouldn't get it if he did.
There is gas and coals and vittles, and the house-rent falling due,
   And it's more than rather likely there's a kid.
There are girls he walked with casual, they'll be sorry now he's gone,
   For an absent-minded beggar they will find him,
But it ain't the time for sermons with the winter coming on—
   We must help the girl that Tommy's left behind him!
*Cook's son—Duke's son—son of a belted Earl—
   Son of a Lambeth publican—it's all the same to-day!
Each of 'em doing his country's work (and who's to look after the
   girl?)
Pass the hat for your credit's sake, and—pay! pay! pay!*

There are families by thousands, far too proud to beg or speak—
   And they'll put their sticks and bedding up the spout,
And they'll live on half o' nothing paid 'em punctual once a week,
   'Cause the man that earns the wage is ordered out.
He's an absent-minded beggar, but he heard his country call,
   And his reg'ment didn't need to send to find him:
He chucked his job and joined it—so the job before us all
   Is to help the home that Tommy's left behind him!
*Duke's job—cook's job—gardener, baronet, groom—
   Mews or palace or paper-shop—there's some one gone away!
Each of 'em doing his country's work (and who's to look after the
   room?)
Pass the hat for your credit's sake, and—pay! pay! pay!*

Let us manage so as, later, we can look him in the face,
   And tell him—what he'd very much prefer—
That, while he saved the Empire his employer saved his place,
   And his mates (that's you and me) looked out for *her.*
He's an absent-minded beggar and he may forget it all,
   But we do not want his kiddies to remind him,
That we sent 'em to the workhouse while their daddy hammered
   Paul,
   So we'll help the homes that Tommy left behind him.

Cook's home—Duke's home—home of a millionaire—
  (Fifty thousand horse and foot going to Table Bay!)
Each of 'em doing his country's work (and what have you got to
    spare?)
Pass the hat for your credit's sake, and—pay! pay! pay!

The Female of the Species

When the Himalayan peasant meets the he-bear in his pride,
He shouts to scare the monster who will often turn aside.
But the she-bear thus accosted rends the peasant tooth and nail.
For the female of the species is more deadly than the male.

When Nag, the wayside cobra, hears the careless foot of man,
He will sometimes wriggle sideways and avoid it if he can,
But his mate makes no such motion where she camps beside the
    trail—
For the female of the species is more deadly than the male.

When the early Jesuit fathers preached to Hurons and Choctaws,
They prayed to be delivered from the vengeance of the squaws—
'Twas the women, not the warriors, turned those stark enthusiasts
    pale—
For the female of the species is more deadly than the male.

Man's timid heart is bursting with the things he must not say,
For the Woman that God gave him isn't his to give away;
But when hunter meets with husband, each confirms the other's
    tale—
The female of the species is more deadly than the male.

Man, a bear in most relations, worm and savage otherwise,
Man propounds negotiations, Man accepts the compromise;
Very rarely will he squarely push the logic of a fact
To its ultimate conclusion in unmitigated act.

Fear, or foolishness, impels him, ere he lay the wicked low,
To concede some form of trial even to his fiercest foe.
Mirth obscene diverts his anger; Doubt and Pity oft perplex
Him in dealing with an issue—to the scandal of the Sex!

But the Woman that God gave him, every fibre of her frame
Proves her launched for one sole issue, armed and engined for the
  same,
And to serve that single issue, lest the generations fail,
The female of the species must be deadlier than the male.

She who faces Death by torture for each life beneath her breast
May not deal in doubt or pity—must not swerve for fact or jest.
These be purely male diversions—not in these her honour dwells—
She, the Other Law we live by, is that Law and nothing else!

She can bring no more to living than the powers that make her great
As the Mother of the Infant and the Mistress of the Mate;
And when Babe and Man are lacking and she strides unclaimed to
  claim
Her right as femme (and baron), her equipment is the same.

She is wedded to convictions—in default of grosser ties;
Her contentions are her children, Heaven help him, who denies!
He will meet no cool discussion, but the instant, white-hot, wild
Wakened female of the species warring as for spouse and child.

Unprovoked and awful charges—even so the she-bear fights;
Speech that drips, corrodes and poisons—even so the cobra bites;
Scientific vivisection of one nerve till it is raw,
And the victim writhes in anguish—like the Jesuit with the squaw!

So it comes that Man, the coward, when he gathers to confer
With his fellow-braves in council, dare not leave a place for her
Where, at war with Life and Conscience, he uplifts his erring hands
To some God of Abstract Justice—which no woman understands.

And Man knows it! Knows, moreover, that the Woman that God gave
  him
Must command but may not govern; shall enthrall but not enslave
  him.
And *She* knows, because She warns him and Her instincts never fail,
That the female of Her species is more deadly than the male!

Notes to the Text

An immense vocabulary, drawn from many historical, social and professional levels of the English language, is one of the characteristics of Kipling's poetry. Hardly any reader will fail to have recourse to a good dictionary now and again. These brief notes concentrate on the Asian and African allusions, British army jargon and a few other specialized geographical and historical terms. No attempt has been made to gloss such items as (to give only two instances) the parts of a ship's engine detailed in "McAndrew's Hymn" (not to mention the Scottish dialect!) or the far-flung topography of "The English Flag."

A LEGEND OF THE FOREIGN OFFICE. "Simpkin": Hindustani pronunciation of champagne. Peg: small drink. C. S. I.: Companion of (the Order of) the Star of India, a high decoration. Cess: tax for special purpose. Bukhshi: commander in chief. Mahratta: a people of central western India. Hookum: order. Dasturi: bribery. Birthday honors: decorations announced on the occasion of the British monarch's birthday. C. I. E.: Companion of (the Order of) the Indian Empire, a lower-ranking decoration. Thana: police station. Lakh: 100,000 rupees. Zenana: harem.

THE STORY OF URIAH. Uriah: husband of Bathsheba, whom King David sent to the front line to get him out of the way. Quetta: in what is now the Pakistani province Baluchistan, in Kipling's day a remote and dangerous post. Simla: Himalayan summer resort town for British officers in India. Screw: pay. Hurnai: Harnai, in the Quetta region.

THE BETROTHED. Suttee: faithful Indian widow who cremates herself on her husband's pyre.

THE BALLAD OF EAST AND WEST. Border: between British India and Afghanistan. Calkins: sharp metal pieces attached to horseshoes for stability; turning them would confuse the trail. Ressaldar: commander of a native cavalry troop. Snaffle: type of bridle bit. Byre: cowshed. Ling: heather. Peshawur: Peshawar, chief border town on the Indian (now Pakistani) side. Khyber: border pass near Peshawar.

THE BALLAD OF THE KING'S MERCY. Durani: Durrani, Afghani tribal confederation. Balkh, Kandahar: provinces of Afghanistan. Kaffir: "unbeliever" in Arabic. Euzufzai: Afghani tribe. Reiver: robber, cattle rustler. Sungar: breastwork. Usbeg: Uzbek, a Central Asian people. Ramazan: Islamic fasting month.

THE BALLAD OF THE 'BOLIVAR.' Hog: receive upward curvature in the keel. Lloyd's: London insurance house.

IN THE NEOLITHIC AGE. Dwerg: dwarf. Solutré, Grenelle: French prehistoric sites. Tr—1: Traill (the mid-nineteenth-century editor of the *Encyclopaedia Britannica*??). Allobrogenses: ancient Gallic tribe. Kew, Clapham: London suburbs. Khatmandhu: capital of Nepal. Martaban: town in Burma.

TOMLINSON. Empusa: ancient Greek hobgoblin.

TOMMY. Tommy Atkins: personification of the British enlisted man. Widow: Queen Victoria.

'FUZZY-WUZZY.' Paythan: Pathan, an Afghani people. Impi: body of warriors. Martini: Martini-Henry rifle. Square: hollow-square battle formation.

GUNGA DIN. Aldershot: military camp near London. Bhisti: water carrier. Dooli: litter, stretcher. Lazarushian-leather: humorous combination of Lazarus and Russian leather.

OONTS. Penk: tap.

MANDALAY. Theebaw: Thibau, king of Burma 1878–1885, conquered by the British. Hathi: elephant.

GENTLEMEN-RANKERS. The title term means rank-and-file soldiers who belonged to the gentry in civilian life.

L'ENVOI (TO 'BARRACK-ROOM BALLADS'). Tents of Shem: connotes comfortable home territory. Peter: signal for setting sail.

SESTINA OF THE TRAMP-ROYAL. Sestina: a poem written to the prosodic rules manifested in this one. Tucker: food, sustenance.

THE LADIES. Prome: town in Burma. 'Oogli: Hugli, town in Bengal. De Castrer: de Castro, typical name of an Anglo-Indian (of mixed Indian and European—in this case, Portuguese—parentage). Neemuch, Mhow: in Central India. Meerut: city near Delhi.

THE SERGEANT'S WEDDIN'. "An' a rogue is married to, etc.": the "etc." stands for "a whore"; the Victorians wouldn't spell it out, but they knew which word was intended. Twig: observe.

THE 'EATHEN. Lance: lance corporal, still drawing private's pay.

THE WHITE MAN'S BURDEN: written 1899, an exhortation to the United States upon its acquisition of the Philippines.

A SONG TO MITHRAS. Mithras: god of an Iranian salvation religion in the early centuries A.D., especially popular with legionaries throughout the Roman Empire. Wall: Hadrian's Wall in the north of England, Rome's northwesternmost frontier.

HADRAMAUTI. Hadramauti: native of a region of what is now Saudi Arabia. Eblis: Satan.

THE VAMPIRE: inspired by a painting by Philip Burne-Jones exhibited in London in 1897.

THE ABSENT-MINDED BEGGAR: written during the Boer War and intended for public performance, it was set to music by Sir Arthur Sullivan. Paul: Kruger, the Boer leader.

THE FEMALE OF THE SPECIES: originally bearing the subtitle "A Natural History," this devastatingly misogynistic piece ironically was first published in the U.S. in *The Ladies' Home Journal*!

Alphabetical List of Titles

page

Absent-Minded Beggar, The	64
Ballad of East and West, The	6
Ballad of the 'Bolivar,' The	12
Ballad of the King's Mercy, The	9
Betrothed, The	4
Blue Roses	61
Boots	53
Cities and Thrones and Powers	54
Conundrum of the Workshops, The	13
Danny Deever	22
'Eathen, The	47
English Flag, The	16
Female of the Species, The	66
'Fuzzy-Wuzzy'	25
Gentlemen-Rankers	33
Gunga Din	27
Hadramauti	56
If—	59
I Keep Six Honest Serving-Men	60
In the Neolithic Age	15
Ladies, The	44
Law of the Jungle, The	57
Legend of the Foreign Office, A	1
L'Envoi [to *Barrack-Room Ballads*] = The Long Trail	

	page
L'Envoi [to *The Seven Seas*] = When Earth's Last Picture Is Painted	
Long Trail, The	35
McAndrew's Hymn	37
Mandalay	32
Mother o' Mine	62
My Rival	3
Oonts	29
Recessional	63
Sea and the Hills, The	50
Sergeant's Weddin', The	46
Sestina of the Tramp-Royal	42
Song of the Little Hunter, The	61
Song to Mithras, A	56
Story of Uriah, The	2
Tarrant Moss	55
Tomlinson	18
Tommy	24
Vampire, The	62
When Earth's Last Picture Is Painted	50
When 'Omer Smote 'Is Bloomin' Lyre	44
White Man's Burden, The	52
Widow at Windsor, The	30

Alphabetical List of First Lines

page

Abdhur Rahman, the Durani Chief, of him is the story told	9
A fool there was and he made his prayer	62
'Ave you 'eard o' the Widow at Windsor	30
By the old Moulmein Pagoda, lookin' eastward to the sea	32
Cities and Thrones and Powers	54
Ere Mor the Peacock flutters, ere the Monkey People cry	61
'E was warned agin' er—	46
God of our fathers, known of old	63
I closed and drew for my love's sake	55
If I were hanged on the highest hill	62
If you can keep your head when all about you	59
I go to concert, party, ball—	3
I keep six honest serving-men	60
In the Neolithic Age savage warfare did I wage	15
I've taken my fun where I've found it	44
I went into a public-'ouse to get a pint o' beer	24
Jack Barrett went to Quetta	2
Lord, Thou hast made this world below the shadow of a dream	37
Mithras, God of the Morning, our trumpets waken the Wall!	56
Now this is the Law of the Jungle—as old and as true as the sky	57
Now Tomlinson gave up the ghost in his house in Berkeley Square	18
Oh, East is East, and West is West, and never the twain shall meet	6

	page
Open the old cigar-box, get me a Cuba stout	4
Roses red and roses white	61
Seven men from all the world, back to Docks again	12
Speakin' in general, I 'ave tried 'em all	42
Take up the White Man's burden—	52
The 'eathen in 'is blindness bows down to wood an' stone	47
There's a whisper down the field where the year has shot her yield	35
This is the reason why Rustum Beg	1
To the legion of the lost ones, to the cohort of the damned	33
We're foot—slog—slog—slog—sloggin' over Africa—	53
We've fought with many men acrost the seas	25
'What are the bugles blowin' for?' said Files-on-Parade	22
When Earth's last picture is painted, and the tubes are twisted and dried	50
When 'Omer smote 'is bloomin' lyre	44
When the flush of a new-born sun fell first on Eden's green and gold	13
When the Himalayan peasant meets the he-bear in his pride	66
When you've shouted "Rule Britannia," when you've sung "God save the Queen"—	64
Who hath desired the Sea?—the sight of salt water unbounded—	50
Who knows the heart of the Christian? How does he reason?	56
Winds of the World, give answer! They are whimpering to and fro—	16
Wot makes the soldier's 'eart to penk, wot makes him to perspire?	29
You may talk o' gin and beer	27